The
Lost Beers & Breweries
of BRITAIN

BRIAN GLOVER

AMBERLEY

About the Author

Brian Glover is a former Editor of Publications for CAMRA, the Campaign for Real Ale. He has written many books on beer including *The World Encyclopedia of Beer*, *Brewing for Victory* on the brewing industry during World War II and the *New Beer Guide* on Britain's craft brewery revolution.

First published 2012

Amberley Publishing
The Hill, Stroud
Gloucestershire, GL5 4EP

www.amberleybooks.com

Copyright © Brian Glover 2012

The right of Brian Glover to be identified as the Author
of this work has been asserted in accordance with the
Copyrights, Designs and Patents Act 1988.

British Library Cataloguing in Publication Data.
A catalogue record for this book is available from the British Library.

ISBN 978 1 4456 0261 5

Typeset in 10pt on 12pt Sabon.
Typesetting and Origination by Amberley Publishing.
Printed in the UK.

Contents

Introduction

Some beers bring a smile to people's lips, years after they last drank them. When I found a 1936 advert for Barclay's Russian Stout in a box of old magazines, the bookshop owner's tired eyes lit up. 'There was no rushing a Russian,' he said with a grin. 'And if you had more than two bottles you struggled to stand up.' As the advert for the stout claimed, 'This'll make you tingle' and 'feel warmed to the marrow'. It certainly lifted one old man's spirits that day, decades after it was last brewed.

Many people remember their first beer. The taste lingers in the memory like their first kiss. Perhaps they puckered up their face in disgust, as it tasted so bitter compared to the sugary pop of childhood. But then came that golden moment when we discovered a drop that really tickled our taste buds. That tentative sip, a tingle on the tongue, a swirl round the mouth and a lick of the lips. Then the first swallow, followed by a summer of pint after pint. Or if it was Russian Stout, one bottle.

But how many of these beers are still pouring today? And even if the brand still exists in name, it may be just a pale shadow – a ghost of a once larger-than-life character. It may have lost all links with the home it once haunted. And that is important. For our perception of a beer is often linked to a place – a much-loved pub or where we were born or once lived. There's a solid liquid bond between such beers and their drinkers. It's more than just taste. It's pure emotion.

For me, growing up in Leeds, Carlsberg's closure in 2011 of Tetley's brewery near the centre of the city meant the heart had been torn out of my local brew. Tetley's Bitter had been my youth, my home town, in a glass. Carlsberg had smashed the glass. On brewing days I used to smell the mash in the air, while their huge Shire horses were such a welcome feature of the streets that, when the council contemplated restricting them in 1971, after a driver complained that the plodding drays held up traffic, the *Yorkshire Evening Post* was deluged with letters backing the gentle giants.

A 'Tetley Bitter' is still produced, but it is no longer brewed in Leeds or even in Yorkshire, but in Wolverhampton. No matter how many tasting trials were carried out, no matter how well matched it was to the original recipe, it is no longer the local brew. Its roots have been torn up and trampled. When I return home, I will not seek out a pint. It's now just another contract brand. Tetley's huntsman has lost its head – and its soul.

I suspect that feeling is shared by Boddingtons drinkers across the Pennines. It was once the city's golden brew – 'The Cream of Manchester' – until it was taken over by Whitbread in 1989 and then swallowed by another international combine. Campaign for Real Ale founder Michael Hardman recalled, 'One expatriate northerner I worked with in London in the early 1970s even named her cat Boddington to evoke fond memories of the misspent evenings of her youth. Boddingtons was one of the flavours of the decade.'

When InBev closed the Strangeways Brewery in 2005, a local commented, 'Boddingtons has been part of our heritage for generations. We just want InBev to leave it alone.' But the axe fell and now the brewery chimney only towers over a wind-swept car park. At least the distinctive cask bitter was still brewed in Manchester by Hyde's in Moss Side – until InBev decided in 2010 to dispose of the brand and end the contract.

Similarly in London, Young's Bitter and Special have lost their local sparkle after the company announced in 2006 that it was selling off its valuable Ram Brewery site in Wandsworth. The capital's drinkers were shocked. 'Young's, like its best bitter, is special. It's stood there in the middle of Wandsworth for so long that it's part of the landscape. A given. You just can't imagine it not being there,' wrote editor Ted Bruning in the CAMRA national newspaper *What's Brewing*. Its chairman John Young, who died that year, had been one of the campaign's early heroes when he defied the industry's switch from traditional cask to processed keg beer. But the Ram was still slaughtered and Young's 'London' beers are now brewed in Bedford.

But these lost leaders left a gaping gap in the market. In Yorkshire, the Leeds Brewery, founded in 2007, saw demand for its Leeds Pale and Best shoot up. The company had held a Goodbye Tetley's beer festival in the week Tetley's closed. 'We're incredibly proud to be picking up the mantle and continuing the great tradition of brewing here in Leeds,' said director Sam Moss. He was soon joined in the city by other ventures like Wharfebank, Kirkstall and Ridgeside, with Tetley's former head brewer Ian Smith in charge of brewing at Wharfebank in an old paper mill.

In Manchester, while Boddingtons brewery has gone, new ventures also frothed up to join the surviving family businesses of Hyde's and Holt's. One, Boggart Hole Clough, named after a local park, is brewing on the site of another fallen giant, Wilson's of Newton Heath, which closed in 1987 after being taken over by Watney's of London. The capital's drinkers have also welcomed a surge of new breweries in recent years, notably Sambrook's, founded in Battersea in 2008, after City accountant Duncan Sambrook decided to stop moaning about the loss of Young's and do something to satisfy the thirst for local beer.

The 2012 *Good Beer Guide* recorded that a staggering ninety-nine breweries had opened across the UK in the previous twelve months, bringing the total to 840. This compared to a total of just 150 breweries in the 1975 guide, after a tidal wave of takeovers in the 1960s had closed many plants to create the 'Big Six' national combines of Allied Breweries (Ansells, Ind Coope and Tetley-Walker), Bass Charrington, Courage, Scottish & Newcastle, Watney-Mann and Whitbread.

A quarter-of-a-century before then in 1949, the Brewers' Society had been trying to reassure drinkers, in a series of 'Beer is Best' adverts, that 'there are more than 2,000 different and distinctive beers brewed every week by over 500 brewers in this country. There *is* a wide choice'. But this was nothing compared to the start of the century. In 1900, the total number of breweries in the UK, including many home-brew pubs, had been 6,447. Areas like the Black Country were known for their large number of home-brew houses. They also persisted in some major towns like Preston, Derby and, despite Tetley's later dominance, Leeds.

The twentieth century was an era of constant contraction until the final decades. Choice at the bar was slowly squeezed dry, until in some areas like Norfolk, one brewer (Watney's) dominated the region. National processed keg brands like Double Diamond, Worthington E, Tavern, Tankard, Tartan and Red Barrel elbowed out many local traditional brews.

The tide began to turn after the arrival of CAMRA in the 1970s. For the first time brewery closures, like Joule's in Staffordshire, were challenged with marches and demonstrations. At the same time new breweries began to appear. Martin Sykes, who was behind the first new independent brewing company for fifty years – Selby Brewery in 1972 – was also a member of the first CAMRA National Executive. Bill Urquart, who had been made redundant by Watney's when they closed Phipps Northampton Brewery, set up his own Litchborough Brewery in 1974. Slowly the fresh barrel began to roll, led by another casualty from the bigger brewers, Peter Austin, the head brewer of Hull Brewery until it was taken over by Northern Foods in 1975. He acted as a consultant to many of the new concerns.

Meanwhile the Big Six national brewers were in turn swallowed by even larger global giants with even less regard for local brewing heritage. They just wanted to promote their international lagers like Stella Artois, Budweiser and Carlsberg. The last of the six, Scottish & Newcastle, was taken over by Heineken in 2008. S&N had already closed its Newcastle Brewery in 2004, moving production to the former clubs Federation Brewery across the river. Newcastle Brown became 'Gateshead Broon'. Then the famous bottled beer lost all ties with the Tyne when Heineken closed the Dunston plant in 2010. Brewing moved again, this time to John Smith's of Tadcaster in North Yorkshire. Newcastle Brown is now 'Taddy Brown' despite the name on the label.

But many of the older breweries and their beers are not forgotten. Some have been revived by new brewing ventures. At least four different versions of Barnsley Bitter have been brewed since the Barnsley Brewery closed in 1976, such is the local affection for the popular beer. This book aims to tickle your taste buds about other lost brews – some of which have also been brought back from the dead.

This'll make you tingle

For hours after you've drunk a Barclay's Russian Stout you feel warmed to the marrow. This is the potent 'vintage' stout that gladdened the heart of the Russian Court 150 years ago. Order a good supply now and keep yourself well stocked throughout the winter to strengthen you and keep you up to the mark.

Barclay's
RUSSIAN STOUT

Matured at least a year in bottle — and goes on maturing

1. Barclay's Russian Stout could still cause a tingle decades after it was last brewed.

ENGLAND

BEER: Allsopp's India Pale Ale
BREWER: Samuel Allsopp & Sons, Burton-on-Trent
ALSO KNOWN FOR: Allsopp's Lager and John Bull
BREWERY LOGO: A red hand
HISTORIC RIVAL: Bass Pale Ale
SIMILAR BREWS TODAY: Marston's Old Empire (5.7%) from Burton-on-Trent
ILLUSTRATIONS: 7, 65-8

ALLSOPP'S IPA: It was a cry from the heart. Allsopp's chairman Sir William Barclay Peat, founder of accountants Peat Marwick, had been trying for years to restore the fortunes of Burton brewers Allsopp's, after being appointed receiver in 1911. He told the AGM in 1925:

> Allsopp's were the pioneers of India Pale Ale, and did a great deal of business with India in that particular brew, but all the advantages which we possess as the oldest existing brewers in Burton ... have dwindled.
>
> Our great mistake was to forget to push the pale ale trade ... and to substitute for it lager beer, which was never anything but a heavy loss and a source of difficulty in the way of progress with what was our natural output, pale ale.

Allsopp's fall from eminence had been dramatic. When the company had been floated in 1887, its £3.3 million shares had been oversubscribed thirty-seven times. Everyone wanted a piece of the famous name. Even the future King Edward VII visited the brewery. Yet within three years it had become a laughing stock. Chairman Lord Hindlip (Samuel Charles Allsopp) was depicted in a cartoon on the cover of *City Life* magazine being thrown out of the offices of the London and Westminster Bank. Under the title 'Poor Old Allsopp!' the bank director tells the dumped brewer, 'I can't have you here ... you've fallen so low, I must really ask you to go away!'

The company dated back to 1742 when Benjamin Wilson took over the Blue Stoops pub and brewhouse in Burton High Street – and expanded. As the first major Burton brewer, he built his reputation not on bitter pale ales but on sweetish darker brews, which were exported to the Baltic from Hull. Peat claimed the Tsar of Russia, Peter the Great, was a customer. In 1807 his son's nephew, Samuel Allsopp, took control and within a year was asking customers 'whether pale ale or that of a darker colour is most liked?'

IPAs were developed in London from stock ales in the eighteenth century, notably by George Hodgson in Bow. He built up a substantial trade supplying the ships of the East India Company. But when the brewery in 1821 tried to ship the beer themselves, the company invited Allsopp, whose exports to Russia had been hit by high taxes, to brew an IPA.

Allsopp's maltster Job Goodhead later claimed that they first experimented making this heavily-hopped beer in a teapot. It proved a success, as Burton's hard, mineral-rich water was better suited to this style than London's. And out of the legendary little teapot poured a vast business.

Soon Allsopp and rivals Bass were the masters of the pale ale trade in India and, after the arrival of the railways in Burton in 1839, at home as well. The beers were produced using the Burton Union system, with fermentation in extensive rows of linked casks. Trade tripled every ten years. A new brewery built next to the railway station in 1859 covered 50 acres. It was regarded as one of the marvels of the age. Its own internal rail system ran for 11 miles.

But success went to the family's head. Samuel's son Henry bought a mansion in Hindlip, Worcestershire, and became the local MP. His sons acquired their own country seats and married into the aristocracy. The family took their eyes off the bread-and-butter beer business. They failed to appreciate the threat from the growing tied-house system, as rivals bought up pubs. They thought the revered Allsopp's name would still sell itself, but brewers across the country began to produce cheaper pale ales. Some London firms like Mann's, Truman and Charrington established breweries in Burton in order to compete. By the 1880s Allsopp's sales were on the slide, though this was not revealed in the share prospectus.

The situation was exacerbated by Allsopp's being grossly overcapitalised. They had sold far too many shares and the profits could not cover the charges and dividends. When shareholders at a noisy 1890 AGM asked how much the Allsopp family would give back from the fortune they had pocketed, Lord Hindlip replied, 'Not a damn penny', before striding off the platform and resigning as chairman.

The company staggered from one crisis to another over the next twenty years. Percy Allsopp, who became chairman in 1895, tried desperate measures, including a late, reckless rush to buy up over-priced pubs – funded by issuing more shares. He even ventured into the entertainment business, snapping up Essex's answer to Blackpool's Winter Gardens, the Southend Kursaal.

He also switched the emphasis of production from the powerful IPA (1060 OG), by installing an American-style lager plant in Allsopp's old brewery in 1899. Unfortunately, he was decades ahead of his time and sales failed to take off despite extensive advertising. 'Lager never amounted to more than 40,000 barrels and Allsopp's became so associated with lager in the public's mind that their pale ale trade was virtually thrown away, leaving a bulk of less profitable mild,' said Allied Breweries former head of research Ray Anderson in *The Fall of the House of Allsopp*.

After Percy Allsopp's resignation in 1900, the company limped on, seeking sanctuary in a merger with local rivals like the Burton Brewery Company and Salt's. But despite lengthy talks nothing materialised. Eventually, the inevitable happened. Allsopp's went into receivership in 1911. The house of Allsopp had crashed – only to rise again.

The receiver William Peat made an inspired choice of managing director in John Calder. The experienced brewery manager from Alloa revived the company's fortunes, before merging with next-door Burton neighbours Ind Coope in 1934. But by then Allsopp's IPA only accounted for 2% of production and it was soon eclipsed by Ind Coope's sparkling pale ale brand – Double Diamond. Allsopp's was dropped from the company title in 1959, though the name was retained for export lagers and later briefly revived at home in the 1980s for Samuel Allsopp's Gold Cross cask lager.

ODD BUT TRUE: The Allsopp family seat, Hindlip Hall in Worcestershire, was a potential home for the War Cabinet in 1940, before becoming the headquarters of West Mercia Police.

BEER: Alton Pale Ale
BREWER: The Alton Brewery, Hampshire
ALSO KNOWN FOR: Hampshire Ale and Double Courage
BREWERY LOGO: The Courage cockerel eclipsed Hall's sun image after 1903
HISTORIC RIVAL: Crowley's Alton Ale
SIMILAR BREWS TODAY: Alton's Pride from the Triple fff Brewery of Four Marks, near Alton, founded in 1997. This was the Supreme Champion Beer of Britain in 2008.
ILLUSTRATIONS: 4, 5, 69-72

ALTON PALE ALE: Burton-upon-Trent may have been the capital of brewing in Britain, but there were other notable centres and Alton in Hampshire was on the 'A' list. It was here in the eighteenth century that one of the early scientific brewers, James Baverstock, developed the use of the hydrometer for measuring beer strength. Thackeray, in his novel *Vanity Fair* in 1847, tells of Joseph Sedley's journey from Southampton to London: 'At Alton he stepped out of the carriage at his servant's request, and imbibed some of the ale for which the place is famous.' Like Burton, it had ideal water for brewing pale ales – unlike London.

Courage had to buy in its pale ales from Fremlins of Maidstone in Kent, with the beer shipped by barge up the Thames. But by the twentieth century it was looking to own its own pale ale brewery. Alton ales were already well known in the capital 40 miles away, as not only did Hall's Alton Brewery own pubs in London, but its local rival across Turk Street, Crowley's, had pioneered city luncheon bars, popularly known as 'Alton ale shops', where workers could enjoy a glass of Alton beer and a ham sandwich for 4d.

The thirst for Alton Pale Ale was considerable; brewed using local Hampshire hops and barley, as well as the town's excellent well water, drawn from the area's chalk belt and claimed to be 'the finest in the country for brewing bitter'. The Alton Brewery, dating back to the eighteenth century, had been bought by Henry Hall in

1841 from John Hawkins. Hall's sons built up the business to 20,000 barrels a year and seventy-seven pubs before Courage made them an offer they couldn't refuse in 1903. It was the London brewer's first takeover outside the capital.

A 1911 price list shows the beer in bottle selling at the same price as Courage's KKK strong ale, with three different qualities on draught. But not all Courage licensees embraced Alton ale. Some preferred the better-known brews from Burton. In 1925 Courage had to send out a letter to thirty-four publicans stating, 'We find on going through our books that your trade in Worthington in bottle is very large compared with your sales of Alton Pale Ale. We should be obliged if you would use your best endeavours to promote the sale of our own beer, which is giving every satisfaction in our houses.'

Courage considerably extended the brewery so that by the 1930s it was brewing ten times the amount of beer produced by the Halls – around 200,000 barrels a year. This had been boosted by taking over Farnham United Breweries in 1927 and concentrating production at Alton. The brewery even had its own railway siding. At its peak in 1950, a quarter-of-a-million barrels were rolled out.

When the London brewer chalked up fifty years in the town, it marked the anniversary with a special Celebration Ale. Chairman Lt-Colonel J. H. Courage came down in March 1954 to pull a lever to release the heavy brew from the copper into the hop-back. It's a wonder it moved, as it was brewed with much more malt and hops than usual.

About eighty barrels were produced of the beer with a mighty original gravity of 1110 (over 10% alcohol), compared to the 1041 strength (4%) of draught Alton Pale Ale or Alton Bitter, as it was by then known. Second brewer Mr G. B. Holland told the *Hampshire Herald* it was 40 degrees stronger than strong Alton Ale (Courage's KKK). The duty on each barrel was a staggering £34, almost five times the £7 and 15s levied on a cask of mild.

The newspaper report added, 'After 10 days fermentation it would be run into specially selected and shaved down hogsheads (large 54-gallon casks) where it would remain for a year before being put into special bottles and sealed with wax. It would be ready for use about Christmas 1955. The beer will not be sold, but kept for special occasions.'

While the strength of draught Alton Bitter had declined over the years, the bottled Alton IPA was largely maintained. Andrew Campbell, in his 1956 *The Book of Beer*, describes it as 'a fine, dry pale ale'. Like Bass, it was sold in two forms, signalled by the colour of the label. Alton Red was still naturally conditioned while Alton Blue was a filtered version. Being matured, Alton Red was seen as a more premium product and was sold at a penny more a half-pint bottle than the Blue. In 1954 the filtered version was revamped and relaunched as John Courage Alton IPA and later just John Courage IPA.

Alton's distinct identity was disappearing, particularly once Courage merged with London rivals Barclay in 1955 and then Simonds of Reading, another noted pale ale brewer, in 1960. The latter merger was celebrated in true English style with a cricket match between the rival tenants at the Alton brewery ground, but the plant was on its final innings. Brewing ceased at Alton in 1969, the last brew being John Courage on 31 May. Production moved to Reading. The following year its historic rival Crowley's opposite also brewed its last, having been taken over by Watney's of London in 1947.

The Alton site continued as a packaging centre for another decade. But brewing did not disappear from the local air, as Guinness, in partnership with other brewers, including Courage, had established its Harp Lager brewery in the town in 1962. This plant was later sold to Bass who extended operations over the old Alton Brewery site in 1980. It is still run today, now owned by international giants Molson Coors.

But a more heady reminder of Alton's brewing history can still be found on the bar. For, according to legend, the Courage directors liked Alton Red so much that they persuaded the head brewer to put some in cask just for them to enjoy. Boardroom guests also sampled the brew and its reputation spread, prompting licensees to demand a drop. Eventually it appeared in a few pubs under the name Alton IPA. 'But locals knew this was the beer the brewery directors drank and one publican produced his own hand-written sign "Directors Bitter". The name stuck', claimed a 1981 advert.

This rich malty reminder of Alton's heritage is still brewed today, now by Wells and Young's of Bedford, who took control of the Courage brands in 2007.

ODD BUT TRUE: Cardinal Newman often stayed in the Alton brewer's house, as a relative, James Newman Frost, was the brewery manager when John Hawkins owned the firm. In contrast, the dark demon of the occult, Aleister Crowley, was a notorious member of the rival brewing family. Its brewery emblem was a black crow's head.

BEER: Arctic Ale
BREWER: Samuel Allsopp, Burton-on-Trent
ALSO KNOWN FOR: Allsopp's Lager, IPA and John Bull
BREWERY LOGO: A red hand
HISTORIC RIVAL: Polar Ale, Abington Brewery, Northampton
SIMILAR BREWS TODAY: Charter Ale (10% abv) from Elveden Ales, Thetford, Norfolk - the recipe is based on the original Arctic Ale which accompanied Belcher's 1852 expedition from Harwich. For a more powerful blast try Global Arctic Warmer (15%) from North Cotswold Brewery.
ILLUSTRATIONS: 6, 73-4

ARCTIC ALE: For once a beer name that was not dreamed up by branding consultants, but with a real heritage, firmly frozen in time. In 1852 Admiral Belcher set sail for the Arctic. His mission was to find Sir John Franklin, who had disappeared in 1845 while searching for a sea route around the top of North America – the legendary Northwest passage.

To try to ensure that Belcher's expedition did not suffer Franklin's chilling fate, the Government in 1851 asked Samuel Allsopp's of Burton to brew a special ale fit for the polar regions. Allsopp's had been chosen because it had been the first British brewery to set up a laboratory in 1845. The result was Arctic Ale, a glowing dark ruby red beer with built-in anti-freeze. It was so strong, it was claimed that the thick wort would not run through the tap during brewing, but had to be 'lifted out with buckets'.

Allsopp's Arctic Ale was launched at the Royal Harwich Yacht Club in 1852, from where the expedition set out. The warming barley wine, with a flavour like old Madeira, was an instant success with the frost-bitten crew. Belcher reported to the Admiralty that 'it has indeed been a great blessing to us, particularly for our sick. It kept exceedingly well and was sought-after by all'.

The rich brew proved the perfect antidote for the constant scourge of sailors, scurvy, as it contained a large amount of unfermented extract, providing a nourishing food as well as a drink. Despite its high alcohol content, it did at times partially freeze, forcing out the bottle-stoppers. But once the 'semi-frozen spongy mass' had been thawed out and re-bottled, it proved just as good as ever. A polar star was born.

The bottle-conditioned beer accompanied further expeditions, including Sir Leopold McLintock's venture of 1857, which discovered the remains of Franklin's ill-fated party. Sir George Nares reported in 1875 that the brew retained its quality in temperatures of 93 degrees below freezing. It was described as being 'as mellow as old Burgundy and as nourishing as beef steak'. Brewery chronicler Alfred Barnard, on a visit to Allsopp's in 1889, tried a bottle of the 1875 brew and said it had a 'vinous, nutty flavour'. The original gravity was 1130, giving a staggering alcohol content of 11.25%.

But the sustaining drop could not keep Allsopp's afloat, despite proving popular in some surprising markets, notably the West Indies. One of Burton-on-Trent's great family brewing dynasties, the company ran into financial difficulties before the First World War and went into receivership. Eventually it combined with local rival Ind Coope in 1934, and its name slowly faded away.

But despite the stormy financial waters, Arctic Ale was still going strong with bold sailors a century after it was first brewed. Stanley Smith, who crossed the Atlantic in 1951 in his 20-foot sloop *Nova Scotia*, took crates with him to help him over the waves.

By then Ind Coope had taken over the beer, and was promoting nip bottles in colourful full-page magazine adverts as the brew which 'keeps out the cold'. In a bid to broaden its market, promotions proclaimed, 'Today Arctic Ale is not only enjoyed by the adventurous. More and more people at home appreciate its encouraging strength and mellow, smooth flavour. Try some yourself on a winter's day.' Arctic Ale was even sold as a Christmas six-pack, with leaflets giving recipes for Arctic pudding and a powerful beer punch.

However, not enough drinkers followed the warming advice. Sightings of the brew soon became as rare as a polar bear on the Thames. 'Strong ales have a limited public,' lamented Andrew Campbell in his 1956 *Book of Beer*. He struggled to find a bottle in the pubs. 'The barmaid at a large, well-run establishment in the East End of London, asked for a strong ale, proposed best bitter or Burton. It took some questioning to discover that the brewery had a barley wine.' Shops were no better. Mr Campbell even tried the wine counter of a large department store. 'There was much searching and ferreting in the rear part of the store until a bottle of Ind Coope & Allsopp's Arctic Ale was eventually produced.'

The beer with an old sailing ship on the label was heading for the rocks once Ind Coope became part of Allied Breweries in the early 1960s. Rich barley wines were seen as old-fashioned ales by the thrusting combine, which put its marketing muscle behind keg Double Diamond and Skol lager. In 1970 they replaced the heavy drop with a lighter, drier brew called Triple A. Arctic Ale had hit its final iceberg.

ODD BUT TRUE: The Arctic name was brought out of deep freeze in 1977 for Allied's thin, low-calorie lager, Arctic Lite. It only lasted a few years before being switched off.

BEER: Audit Ale
BREWER: Lacon's, Great Yarmouth, Norfolk
ALSO KNOWN FOR: Old Nogg and Old XXXX Ale
BREWERY LOGO: A falcon
HISTORIC RIVAL: Greene King of Bury St Edmunds, near Cambridge, continued to brew an Audit 'barley wine' (OG 1074-80) into the 1980s.
SIMILAR BREWS TODAY: Blackfriars Brewery of Great Yarmouth, established in 2004, brew an occasional Audit Ale (8% abv) to the original Lacon's recipe. Kelham Island of Sheffield also brewed just fifty bottles of a 10.7% Audit Ale in 2009, leading to the establishment of an annual Sheffield University Audit Feast.
ILLUSTRATIONS: 8-10, 75

AUDIT ALE: Historically drunk by tenant farmers at the gathering to pay their annual rent to their feudal landlords. The tradition persisted at the feasts marking the auditing of college accounts at Oxford and Cambridge universities. They were originally brewed by the college's own breweries (see Chancellor Ale, Queen's College, Oxford), but later by commercial breweries, notably Mitchells & Butlers of Birmingham for Oxford and Lacon's for Cambridge.

Combining business and beer was seen as a happy way of sealing a deal. A Frenchman visiting a Cambridge college in 1672 spoke of the need to down 'two or three pots of beer during our parley; for no kind of business is transacted in England without the interaction of pots of beer'.

But only 'the very best ale' was expected at the annual college celebrations. Audit ales were traditionally brewed in October for the feast in January or February. Often casks were laid down in the cellar for a year or more, having been heavily dry-hopped. Sometimes they were spiced or blended with Burgundy and served with 'a hedgehog' – a lemon or orange bristling with cloves – floating in the bowl.

Statesman Sir George Trevelyan, who was a student at Trinity College, Cambridge, in the late 1850s, said, 'Connoisseurs treat audit ale like claret, and place it for a while in front of the fire. But the effect is seldom ascertained for the corks ... almost invariably leap from the bottles and are followed by the best part of the ale.'

Such carelessness was a criminal waste. An American visitor to Trinity in the early 1880s marvelled at its audit ale, saying it was 'as smooth as oil, sweet as milk, clear as amber and strong as brandy' with 'a mingled richness and delicacy of flavour'. He concluded, 'Such a product of malt and hops had never passed my lips before.'

Trinity was the most celebrated as it distributed bottles during the nineteenth century, with college fellows given an allowance of six dozen a year. John Bickerdyke sang its praises in *The Curiosities of Ale and Beer* in 1889: 'Trinity Audit is as superior to all other mortal brews as Chateau Lafite is to *vin ordinaire*.'

But the expense and trouble of brewing on the premises saw most college breweries close, including Trinity's in 1890. By the 1920s commercial breweries had largely taken over, with Lacon's winning the contracts to supply the majority of Cambridge colleges. Its success, despite being some distance from the university, was due to it having taken over two breweries in Cambridge in the 1890s – plus the fame of its Yarmouth Strong Ale or Old XXXX.

Founded in 1640 and bought by the Lacon family in 1760, the company had a long history of its own and in the nineteenth century had a substantial mild trade in London, where it once owned fifty pubs. The Wrestlers pub at the brewery gates was where Nelson dined after landing at Yarmouth following his defeat of Napoleon at the Battle of the Nile in 1798. The Admiral was escorted by the local yeomanry under Captain E. K. Lacon.

Such colourful anecdotes helped an enterprising graduate briefly export Trinity Audit Ale in champagne quart bottles to New York in 1937, with Lacon's head brewer Edward Taplin promoted as 'a leading authority on audit ale'.

Local brewers like Dale's in Cambridge and Morrell's in Oxford also picked up college audit accounts, while breweries further from the two thirsty centres of learning tried to profit from the famous name. Friary of Guildford in Surrey, Westerham in Kent and Wethered's in Buckinghamshire all produced an audit ale for general sale. Crowley's of Alton in Hampshire, which was once famous for its Vatted Old Ale, also supplied Cambridge colleges.

But by the late 1960s most colleges had switched to wine and port for their big dinner dates and audit ale faded from their high tables. But Lacon's continued to sell its Audit Ale to the public in small 'nip' bottles and in corked and wired pint bottles.

In 1966 it even got its bottles back on a top table. It produced a special Audit Ale for a ball at the Dorchester Hotel in London to mark the centenary of the Government's Exchequer and Audit Department. But by then it had just been taken over by London brewing giants Whitbread, and Lacon's brewing account was closed within two years.

ODD BUT TRUE: Westerham Brewery's Audit Ale (OG 1065) was so well regarded that it was regularly delivered to Sir Winston Churchill's nearby home Chartwell Manor – and to the Queen Mother's residence Clarence House in London. The original Black Eagle Brewery, run by Bushell, Watkins & Smith, ceased brewing in 1965. But a new Westerham Brewery, founded in 2004, revived its Audit Ale, using the original yeast, water source and recipe, brewed to the 1938 strength of 6.2%.

BEER: Barnsley Bitter
BREWER: Barnsley Brewery, Barnsley, South Yorkshire
ALSO KNOWN FOR: Old Tom and Oakwell Stout
BREWERY LOGO: A well below an oak tree or an acorn
HISTORIC RIVAL: Darley's IPA from Thorne, near Doncaster
SIMILAR BREWS TODAY: Acorn and Oakwell Barnsley Bitter
ILLUSTRATIONS: 11, 12, 76, 77

BARNSLEY BITTER: Guy Senior, one of the founders of the Oakwell Brewery in Barnsley, was the Jeremy Clarkson of the Victorian era. He was determined to speed ahead with his business at any cost – as revealed by a poster discovered in an attic.

Alongside busts of railway pioneers George Stephenson and Joseph Locke, it boasts, 'Coal and Iron England's Greatest Wealth' – 'Working Men England's Greatest Strength' – 'No More Bad Trade at Home' – 'No More Horse Corn from Abroad'. Below, two traction engines pulled wagons of beer, one steaming outside the Industry Inn, the other thundering through the country above more muscular mottoes: 'Steam Versus Horses' – 'Traction Engines' – 'Home Production' – 'Work for the Million'.

Peer carefully at the traction engine flying through the fields and you'll spot a policeman crouching in the bushes about to trap the reckless driver – for rumbling along at over four miles an hour without a man walking ahead waving a warning flag.

Yorke Crompton reveals in his 1960 company history *Seventy Years and More*, 'Many times the Seniors were fined for allowing their driver to rush through Yorkshire at this hair-raising pace. Guy Senior welcomed the court cases and the fines, for they proved the enterprise of the brewery in keeping ahead of the times with such rapid deliveries.'

Paul and Guy Senior had been brought up in the brewing trade, their father Seth having founded a celebrated brewery at Shepley, near Huddersfield, known for its Yorkshire Stingo strong ale. Striking out on their own, they set up their brewery in 1858 in the heart of the South Yorkshire coalfield in a former linen bleachworks, alongside Beevor Hall, which became Guy's home and later the brewery's offices.

After his brother died at the early age of thirty-seven in 1863, Guy Senior bought up pubs at a rapid rate. By the time the Barnsley Brewery Company was formed in 1888, he had acquired more than eighty. Ill health had forced him to sell up to a consortium of London businessmen led by Sam Lucas, a Hertfordshire brewer from Hitchin, who became the company's first chairman. But Paul Senior's son Arthur continued to run the business.

The company began to expand further afield, taking over the New Trent Brewery of Crowle in Lincolnshire with thirty pubs in 1918, then hunting down James Fox's 'Tally-Ho Ales', also of Crowle, in 1949, with a further forty houses. One of the New Trent pubs, The Earl of Doncaster in Doncaster, was rebuilt with a bottling plant behind.

But it was the reputation of the draught beers that propelled sales, as chairman Edwin Umbers told the *Financial Times* in 1956: 'The considerable increase in free trade ... reflects the popularity of our beers.' Much of the demand was in working men's clubs. The sherry-coloured Barnsley Bitter was on a growing number of drinkers' lips – and was also being talked about by rival brewers.

The next year a 'trading agreement' was made with John Smith's of Tadcaster, each selling some of the other's beers. But it was much more than that. Smith's also took a share stake in Barnsley and Smith's managing director, W. E. Harbord, joined the board. Barnsley was being drawn into the Magnet brewer's embrace. Four years later John Smith's took complete control of the company and its 240 pubs.

At first the takeover seemed beneficial. Although all bottling was moved to Tadcaster, £1 million was invested in the Oakwell Brewery during the 1960s. Improvements included two new mash tuns, a stainless steel fermenting room and a barrel cleaning store capable of handling 1,000 casks a day, many of them still wooden.

Edwin Umbers planted an oak tree to mark the new era. The brewers celebrated by taking three medals at the Brewex competition in London in 1968. Head brewer Ian Horseman was raising a winning glass again at the next contest at Earl's Court four years later for the dark XXX Mild.

But after John Smith's was taken over by London brewer Courage in 1970, the strategy changed. A traditional draught beer brewery like Barnsley, only 28 miles from Tadcaster, was no longer deemed necessary, as John Smith's turned its back on real ale. In 1973 it was announced that Barnsley was to close. Smith's said the brewery's boilers were packing up and the insurers would not renew coverage. But the cost of replacing them was only a fraction of the £6.5 million being spent on redeveloping Tadcaster.

The Courage group claimed customers would not miss Barnsley Bitter as it would be replaced by John Smith's Bitter. But this was now a processed brew, not a cask beer. Drinkers believed Barnsley Bitter was being dumbed down to ease the switch. CAMRA's 1974 *Good Beer Guide* called BB 'a shadow of its former self'. Columnist Richard Boston in *The Guardian* said, 'Barnsley Bitter, which used to be the boast of Yorkshire for its flavour and strength, has already been considerably weakened.'

In 1974 CAMRA led a lively march through the town. 'Barnsley Bitter is the only thing keeping the town on the map now,' said branch leader John Hatton, after the closure of the local mines. The campaign's national executive was reported to have met at the Red Lion in the morning and sank three firkins – 216 pints – while they drafted a letter of protest to hand in, after the police banned the march from going near the brewery.

Local MP Roy Mason, the Minister of Defence, sent a letter of support and asked the Monopolies Commission to investigate. More than 12,000 people signed a petition. But it was all to no avail. The final brew was on 29 March 1976.

'Thirty years on I can still visualise the beer pumping through the spherical glass electric bar pumps and I haven't forgotten the taste,' CAMRA member Alan Walker recalled. 'We carried the last barrel of Barnsley Bitter from the Leopard down the street. The pub was packed to the rafters just as it was on the last night the beer was on sale at so many other Barnsley Brewery houses.'

Its demise had left a bitter taste – but also a lingering legend that would not die. First to bring back the famous name were two engineers, David Winstanley and Peter Hanby, who set up the Rockside Brewery at Thurlstone in 1984 and then Hoyle Mill, Barnsley, from 1986. Among its beers was Barnsley Bitter (1036). But it folded in 1988.

Then in 1994 the South Yorkshire Brewing Company, led by Mark Hunter, started up at an industrial heritage site at Elsecar, using the original Barnsley yeast. Brewed to a strength of 3.8%, its Barnsley Bitter brought memories flooding back of the rich chestnut beer with a long dry finish. John Smith's was so worried, it tried to stop its licensees stocking the beer. South Yorkshire renamed itself the Barnsley Brewery from 1996, with Robert Umbers of the former ruling family becoming chairman.

The following year, the Oakwell Brewery was set up under former head brewer Ian Horseman on the original Barnsley Brewery site by pub company RBNB, brewing a paler Barnsley Bitter mainly for its thirty-five houses. This resulted in a court clash over the BB name, with Oakwell having to call its brew 'Barnsley Bitter brewed at Oakwell'.

In 2002 the Barnsley Brewery at Elsecar went into liquidation, but its brewer David Hughes soon established the Acorn Brewery in Wombwell, Barnsley, and brewed a Barnsley Bitter again. Just to add to the confusion, the venture at Elsecar continued for a while to market a Barnsley Bitter – brewed in Blackpool. So bewildered drinkers could find three Barnsley Bitters on the bar. Two, from Acorn and Oakwell, are still pouring today. The liquid legend lives on.

ODD BUT TRUE: The Barnsley Brewery Company used to broadcast the prominent letters 'BBC' on its chimney.

BEER: Bass Red Triangle
BREWER: Bass, Burton-on-Trent
ALSO KNOWN FOR: Draught Bass and No. 1 Strong Ale
BREWERY LOGO: A red triangle
HISTORIC RIVAL: Worthington White Shield
SIMILAR BREWS TODAY: Worthington White Shield
ILLUSTRATIONS: 13, 14, 78-80

BASS RED TRIANGLE: 'The Bitter Truth!' shouted the headline in the *Sunday People* in 1972. 'Shock for beer drinkers: Worthy's the same as Bass.' Drinkers of the two bottled pale ales had long argued which was the best. 'Now they can stop swearing by one and scorning the other,' said the newspaper. 'For the two tipples are absolutely identical! Only the labels are different.' It had sent samples for laboratory testing.

The giant Bass Charrington group calmly confessed: 'These two beers have been exactly the same brew for two or three years now. They have been very similar for years. Then it was decided to make both beers absolutely identical,' admitted a spokesman. 'There is no reason why the same beer can't be sold under these two different labels.'

In fact it was four. The traditional bottle-conditioned beer with a sediment was sold as Bass Red Triangle or Worthington White Shield. The brewery-conditioned bright beer, introduced in 1934, was sold as Bass Blue Triangle or Worthington 'E' (Green Shield).

The company was probably relieved that its name game had been exposed. Its marketing of Bass and Worthington had from the late 1950s become remarkably similar. Often they were combined. A 1967 beer mat hinted at the truth, claiming on one side that Worthington 'is equalled only by Bass Red Triangle' and on the other that Bass is 'comparable only with Worthington White Shield'.

After the newspaper revelation, the Red Triangle brand was withdrawn, despite howls of protest from loyal drinkers. It was a bitter irony. The famous beer, whose brewer had filed the UK's first trademark – the Red Triangle – in 1876, and then waged a constant battle against forgeries of its label at home and abroad, had finally succumbed to a copy made by its own company. A certain Arthur Manners must have been quietly cheering in his grave, as Bass launched a major advertising campaign for Worthington White Shield later in 1972 under the slogan 'It takes guts to be original'.

The neighbouring Burton breweries of Bass and Worthington had merged in 1927, but initial plans to combine the running of the companies were thwarted. Worthington's down-to-earth chairman Arthur Manners did not get on with Bass's aristocratic leader John Gretton, and the two businesses continued to operate separately for many years.

Bass, Ratcliff & Gretton was the greater company by far, dating back to 1777. When King Edward VII visited in 1902, it boasted three huge breweries in Burton, producing almost one-and-a-half million barrels a year. The business extended across 750 acres with 17 miles of its own railway track and eleven locomotives. On his visit, Edward VII started a mash of a special strong ale, inevitably called

King's Ale, but when he met the directors, he followed drinkers around the globe by enjoying a glass of Bass Pale Ale.

Though Bass produced a wide variety of beers (there were nineteen different brews in 1866) ranging from barley wines and stouts to milds, it was famed for its pale ale, which was bottled across Britain by other breweries and agencies or sold on draught simply as Bass. It was the beer on which its fortunes had been built, developed from its well-hopped East India Pale Ale, produced for export to the Empire from 1823.

Like all great brands, Bass has many legends to its name. Its introduction to Britain is said to have been by accident, when a shipwreck in the Irish Sea in 1827 led to salvaged casks being sold in Liverpool. In fact, it had been advertised in the UK from the start, but sales only took off after the railway reached Burton in 1839. By 1851, the beer with a gravity of 1065 (7%) had become such an institution that, when Lord Tennyson visited the Great Exhibition in London, the most pressing question on his lips was, 'Can one get a decent bottle of Bass here?' The red triangle, a shipping sign, was adopted in 1855. The brew even boasted its own fan club, the Honourable Order of Bass Drinkers.

Bass attributed its success to three factors – Burton's water with its high gypsum content; only using the best quality malt and hops, and the method of final fermentation, the Burton Union system, which cleansed the ale and ensured its stability. This was vital for the bottle-conditioned Red Triangle. 'Like old wine it forms a crust and care should be taken not to disturb this when decanting,' warned a 1954 Bass booklet. But Red Triangle's prominence had long been disturbed.

Andrew Campbell in his 1956 *Book of Beer* called Bass 'the most renowned draught beer in the world'. He said it now had a gravity of around 1050 'with a fine rich colour and aroma, firm and dry in flavour, strong and mildly bitter to the palate'. But comparing bottled Red Triangle to White Shield, he said, 'Worthington is a little softer and darker than Bass, a little less carbonated, more subtle in flavouring, and therefore perhaps the best choice for the dinner table.' Many were beginning to agree.

Worthington had been a smaller business, but from the 1890s it was much better run and more enterprising than its complacent big brother. After the Second World War, Worthington's ales surged in popularity to the extent that, by 1953, 20% of Bass's own brewing capacity had to be used to brew Worthington beers. In his history of Bass, *The Greatest Brewery in the World*, Colin Owen reveals that between 1949 and 1954 annual sales of bottled Red Triangle fell sharply from 172,000 barrels to 114,000, while White Shield shot up from 125,000 to 191,000. By 1958, the unbelievable had happened. Group sales of Worthington beers exceeded Bass for the first time.

When the company looked to promote a keg beer, it was the Worthington E brand that was chosen to spearhead Bass's challenge in this new market. Bass might be the firm's corporate title, but the beers which carried the famous name were allowed to slide down the bar. Red Triangle fell off the end, while the reputation of Draught Bass, already reduced in strength to 1044 (4.4%), was damaged when in 1980 it was decided to phase out the costly Burton Union system. The Rolls Royce of real ale had become just another Cortina, muttered many drinkers. Sales slipped away.

The stronger White Shield (5.5%) lost its Burton roots in 1990, being brewed in Bass breweries in Sheffield and Birmingham and then by King & Barnes of Sussex. At least when Bass sold out to Belgian giant Interbrew in 2000, it returned home, though the amounts were now so small it could be brewed at the pilot plant at the Bass Museum.

And the beer glass became cloudier after government intervention forced Interbrew to sell Bass's giant Burton brewery to American brewer Coors in 2002 – while retaining the Bass brand. Draught Bass was still brewed in Burton, but from 2005 by Marston's, while Coors took over the museum and the Worthington brands. The long link between Bass and Worthington had been snapped.

But Coors showed faith in White Shield, renaming the Museum Brewery under former Bass brewer Steve Wellington the White Shield Brewery. Sales rose to such an extent that production was moved to the main Burton brewery, while a new £1 million William Worthington Brewery was opened on the museum site in 2010. One of its brews was White Shield on draught. Red Triangle's doppelgänger was fermenting nicely again.

ODD BUT TRUE: Red Triangle was daubed into some famous paintings, including works by Picasso. Manet also immortalised the ale in his painting *A Bar at the Folies-Bergère* in Paris in 1882, with the bottles featured along the counter.

BEER: Carlisle Bitter
BREWER: Carlisle and District State Management Scheme
ALSO KNOWN FOR: Carlisle Mild and Special Export
BREWERY LOGO: None
HISTORIC RIVAL: None
SIMILAR BREWS TODAY: The Derwent Brewery of Silloth, Cumbria, founded in 1996, recreated Carlisle State Bitter (3.7%) using the original recipe, even supplying it to the House of Commons.
ILLUSTRATIONS: 15, 81, 82

CARLISLE BITTER: It was one of the most controversial developments in British brewing history. People's polarised views tended to depend on where they stood politically (or rather sat, since you weren't supposed to stand in Carlisle's pubs). And exactly when they gave their opinion of the fifty-five-year 'experiment' which began as an emergency wartime measure. Though some blamed it on a railway timetable.

During the Great War, a vast munitions factory was built along the Solway Firth, stretching for nine miles. Thousands of navvies were brought in, many from Ireland. With the munitions workers, they totalled more than 20,000. It was well-paid work. After a long day's toil, the train from Gretna to Carlisle arrived in the city five minutes before wartime closing time (pubs were only allowed to open for five-and-a-half hours a day from 1915). Many houses near the station started pulling pints and lining them up on the bar before the thirsty hordes poured in. Boustead's Bar also set out 500 glasses of whisky. Carlisle gained a reputation for drunken mayhem and the vital explosives plant suffered from the hangover. Minister of Munitions Lloyd George determined to stamp out the problem.

In 1916 the Central Control Board (Liquor Traffic), set up to manage Britain's alcohol intake, took over the five breweries in Carlisle and all the pubs in the area. Four were closed with production concentrated at the Old Brewery in Caldewgate. The distant Maryport Brewery was also absorbed as it owned many pubs in Carlisle. This sweeping state control was introduced one year before the Bolshevik Revolution in Russia.

Beer was rationed. At midday a drinker could only have a half. Intoxication was forbidden. An unpopular 'No Treating' order was strictly enforced. Alcohol advertising was banned, as was the local habit of ordering a 'heater and cooler' (a whisky and a pint together). Inspectors were appointed to make sure the rules were obeyed. Pubs that flouted them were ruthlessly shut down. The number in Carlisle plummeted from 119 to 69 by the end of 1918. Off-licences were harder hit, crashing from more than 100 to just 6. Spirit sales were banned on Saturdays from 1917 and pubs were shut on Sundays.

John Hunt in *A City Under the Influence* recalled, 'When you left the pub, the chances are you would have seen a man standing across the road looking for all the world as if he was waiting for a bus. In fact, he was very carefully checking the condition of you and your fellow drinkers. He was an inspector.' Welcome to 1984 – in 1916.

But the drunk did stagger off the streets. Convictions fell from a high of 953 in Carlisle in 1916 to 80 in 1918. When the war ended and most restrictions were lifted, many expected state control to end as well. Instead, power passed in 1921 from the Central Control Board to the Carlisle and District State Management Scheme under the control of the Home Secretary. The Government still wished to pursue the 'experiment'.

Surprisingly there was not a huge outcry, since many supported the more positive aspects of state control. One had been the emphasis on food in pubs as well as drink. Another had been the improvement of basic bars with better seating and facilities. Between the wars this was developed further, as completely new houses were built under the direction of a remarkable architect Harry Redfern.

Large stylish pubs sprang up like the Apple Tree in Lowther Street, built on the site of a former drinking den. Some of Redfern's designs, notably the Crescent Inn in Warwick Road with its balcony, arabesque ironwork and tiling, were considered 'too exotic' for Carlisle, but they inspired the rest of the industry, particularly two breweries.

William Butler, chairman of Mitchells & Butlers of Birmingham, and Sydney Nevile, managing director of London brewing giant Whitbread, had been appointed to the Central Control Board in 1916. They saw the value of much of its work and became leading advocates of improved pubs. Both companies followed Carlisle in building fewer but better houses, with bowling greens, reading rooms and restaurants.

There was just one major complaint. As Sydney Nevile said in his autobiography, *Seventy Rolling Years*, 'Even after 30 years, the complaint is still heard in Carlisle that there is no choice.' Drinkers resented the local monopoly – and after the Second World War, it looked as if state control was about to be extended.

When a radical Labour Government came to power, Home Secretary Herbert Morrison was determined to impose the state management scheme on the new towns being built across the country. But little happened, partly because of determined opposition by the trade, but also because Labour's priorities were nationalising major industries and establishing the NHS. Then Labour lost the 1951 election and the plans were shelved.

During the fierce debate Carlisle was again thrust into the spotlight. The *Sunday Pictorial* described the state houses as offering good beer, a penny a pint cheaper than commercial breweries:

The pubs are very respectable, clean and nice, with poetic quotations on the walls. There is a sort of antiseptic efficiency about them.

Because of this there has been a flight to the clubs, where people can have a sing-song (singing and dancing are banned in Carlisle's pubs) … Another state custom which others may not welcome is the discouragement of drinking at the bars. Customers are asked to sit down. The pubs are efficiently managed – but lack a human touch.

Picture Post complained in 1955, 'Where are the old barmaids? Gone with the wind of state control! And in their stead, subdued figures clothed from head to foot in white overalls. Consequently, when you go to the serving-hatch-grilles to ask for the favour of a drink, you feel that you really ought to be asking for a book of postage stamps'.

But no-one complained about the beer and the Carlisle Brewery steamed quietly ahead. A modern bottling plant was installed in 1956. Carlisle Keg was introduced in 1967. And to answer criticism about lack of choice, beers like Bass, Worthington and Tennent's Lager were made available. But most locals enjoyed their cask Carlisle Mild and Bitter. *Which?* magazine in 1960 said the beers offered excellent value for money. Frank Baillie in *The Beer Drinker's Companion* praised the draught bitter as 'well-flavoured with a good hop rate'.

Then in 1971 Conservative Home Secretary Reginald Maudling dropped his bombshell. The 'experiment' was to be would up. The 172 pubs were sold off, while Theakston's of Yorkshire eventually bought the brewery in 1974.

Head brewer Bill Monk later wrote to the *Cumberland Evening News* that 'the demise of the state scheme had nothing to do with the quality of the beer. In fact it was an embarrassment to close a viable brewery producing high-quality beers at a low price'. The bitter was 11p a pint in 1972 (compared to 13p from most breweries) while the full-bodied dark mild was only 9p. For once a state institution was mourned. People missed state beer – and the low prices.

ODD BUT TRUE: Harry Redfern's assistant, Joseph Seddon, designed a tribute to the architect, the Redfern Inn at Etterby, which opened in 1940 – when the country was again at war.

BEER: Chancellor Ale
BREWER: Queen's College, Oxford
ALSO KNOWN FOR: College Ale
HISTORIC RIVAL: Archdeacon from Merton College, Oxford
SIMILAR BREWS TODAY: None
ILLUSTRATIONS: 16-19, 83

CHANCELLOR ALE: Beer lubricated learning from the start at this famous institution, with a brewer being appointed as early as the college's founding in 1341. The last of Oxford University's college breweries, it was forced to close in the Second World War. Some vessels warped on drying out and production was never revived.

Its strongest and most prestigious brew, Chancellor Ale, was named in honour of a former college member who attained the highest office within the university. It was the most potent of Audit Ales, being brewed once a year in October. The production methods had barely changed for hundreds of years, as recorded in *The Brewers' Journal* in 1927.

A two-and-a-half barrel (90 gallon) brew was made in the usual way, except that the liquor run-off from the first mash was used as the liquor for the second mash, which was also given a fresh charge of malt. This heavyweight double-mash brew – Oxfordshire Museum Services called it 'triple-brewed' in a 1985 booklet – used 50 bushels of malt. It was then boiled for three hours with 20lbs of hops in an open copper and fermented in a round wooden vessel for twenty-four hours before being poured into casks and rolled into an adjoining cellar.

The casks were then set up over yeast troughs to keep fermenting, with the yeast flowing out of the cask into the trough and clean beer being ladled back into the cask, in an early version of the Burton Union system. After six days the beer was run into large upright bell-shaped casks where it matured for two years or longer before being drunk on special occasions in hall from a two-handled silver mug handed around among the fellows and scholars.

It was a potent drop, having a massive original gravity of 1135 (10.7% alcohol by volume). When brewery chronicler Alfred Barnard visited the 50-foot-long stone brewhouse around 1890, he tried some which had been maturing for six years. He declared that two wine glasses would intoxicate a man.

But by 1935, when *The Brewers' Journal* revisited the ancient brewhouse – which had not been substantially rebuilt since the sixteenth century – there were serious signs of decay. Chancellor Ale was now said to be only stored for a year and it was no longer kept in the upright 108-gallon casks as 'these have recently been discarded on account of age'.

The head brewer, J. F. Hunt, who had featured in the 1927 account, had retired after fifty-six years, and there were fears for the future of Chancellor. 'It would be a thousand pities if this magnificent beverage passed out of knowledge with the quaint storage casks which no longer grace the cellar,' said the *Journal*. 'But the tradition is still there and it is hoped that the Chancellor will be revived.'

Even production of the more regular College Ale, which was still brewed to a powerful OG of 1068 (6.6%) had dwindled to thirty barrels a year. This had 'not sufficed for the college thirst' and additional supplies were obtained 'from a well-known Birmingham brewery' (Mitchells & Butlers).

Brewing of Chancellor did eventually stagger on until 1939 thanks to the help of Louis Gunter, second brewer at Morrell's Brewery in Oxford. He was the last to brew Chancellor in what were described as 'virtually museum conditions'. The cleanliness of the old brewhouse was far from ideal and like *Lambic* breweries in Belgium it housed a wealth of micro flora which affected the beer.

Brewing author Lloyd Hind said it had a high level of sourness, containing 0.77% lactic acid. But a three-year-old bottled Chancellor Ale that he tried was still highly drinkable: 'Its flavour, though acid, was wonderfully vinous and pleasant, the acidity being hidden by the buffering colloids of the beer.' The heavyweight recipe, packed with rich malt and bitter hops, balanced out the sourness produced by wild yeasts. It was a drop to savour – but not for long.

After the war the college did begin to refit the brewhouse before abandoning the plan and converting the building into a carpenter's shop. The last chance to revive Chancellor had gone, though Morrell's continued to brew a College Ale (7.4% abv) until its own historic Lion Brewery closed in 1998.

Morrell's had been founded in the late eighteenth century in St Thomas' behind the castle, where the monks of Osney Abbey used to brew. It was one of the few breweries still featuring a water wheel and an open cooling tray. In the 1990s, it even used its history and reputation for strong ales like College and Graduate (5.2%) to try and build an export market in Italy and the USA.

But all the heritage counted for little once the ruling Eld family was forced out. The brewery was shut and the 130 pubs sold off. A drive for higher profits had beaten higher ideals in the academic stronghold.

ODD BUT TRUE: Students at Brasenose College used to drink an Ivy Beer flavoured with ground ivy on Ascension Day every year when they visited neighbouring Lincoln College in atonement for the death of an Oxford student in the sixteenth century.

BEER: Chesters Best Mild
BREWER: Chesters Brewery, Ardwick, Manchester
ALSO KNOWN FOR: Natural Ale and Extra Stout
BREWERY LOGO: A roof cowl and later a brewery tower
HISTORIC RIVAL: Yates' Mild from the Castle Brewery, Ardwick
SIMILAR BREWS TODAY: Holt's Mild from Cheetham, Manchester
ILLUSTRATIONS: 20, 21

CHESTERS BEST MILD: There was nothing meek about Chesters Fighting Mild, as it was known. It sent drinkers staggering out into the streets in search of a scrap, their fists flailing at thin air before they hit the pavement. Or at least that was the legend.

Whitbread, who took over the Threlfall's Chesters group, hinted at this rowdy reputation in their early 1970s marketing of the dark demon, fronted by a busty, pouting barmaid urging customers to 'have a Chesters with the men'.

Beer mats revealed that it packed a hidden punch:

All the things people say about northern beer are especially true about Chesters Best Mild. Much stronger than you'd expect because we give Chesters Best Mild a higher degree of fermentation than most beers ... the blending of toasted malt and caramellised sugar gives its distinctive, rich, deep, glowing brown colour and the taste that's strictly individual. The taste that so many men stay loyal to once they've acquired it, the taste that makes Manchester landlords claim they serve the best beer in Lancashire.

It was fighting talk. But then Chesters had been born in the mean streets of east Manchester. Thomas Chesters was a shopkeeper from Ancoats who went into partnership with brewer Samuel Collins at the small Victoria Brewery in Ardwick before building the larger Ardwick Brewery in Princess Street in 1851. He was soon sole proprietor, buying up pubs in the rapidly growing industrial area before his death in 1872.

His nephew Stephen Chesters Thompson continued to expand, even opening a depot in Walsall before forming a public company in 1888 with eighty-one pubs to raise more capital. This allowed Chesters to buy the Wellington Brewery in Openshaw with twenty-one houses. The confident new company's telegraphic address was simply 'Ale – Manchester'.

Other local breweries soon followed, but the Wellington takeover was to prove most significant for the enterprising young brewer who came with the company. Charles Frederick Hyde did not just supervise the building of a completely new brewery on the Ardwick site from 1903, but after the war he established Chesters' reputation for quality beer and brewing innovation. A qualified chemist, he was continuously experimenting with yeasts, malts and sugars, taking out his first patent in 1911.

In 1920 he introduced a new Best Mild – after years of poor war beer – which soon reigned supreme. Previously Chesters had brewed a range of milds. In 1895, a year after Hyde became head brewer, the company produced a Common Mild selling at 42/- a barrel, a Best Mild at 48/- and a Special Best Mild at 54/-, as well as a Bitter (60/-) and Strong Ale (72/-). The new Best Mild was brewed to Hyde's own formula using a process which he patented the following year. This separated the fine meal in the crushed malt from the coarse grits and then treated the hard grits to make them soluble and so improve malt extraction.

Frank Cowen, who worked for Chesters and later Whitbread West Pennines for more than fifty years, said in his history of the Ardwick Brewery, 'This high gravity beer, henceforward always referred to as Chesters Best Mild, caught the imagination of the drinking public, especially in the heavy industry areas of Openshaw, Gorton, Bradford and Ardwick, where it became affectionately known as "fighting beer" or "lunatic soup". It was to become the company's mainstay throughout its trading life and beyond.'

Charles Frederick Hyde retired from Chesters in 1928 – but did not leave brewing. He had bought the Welcome Brewery in Oldham in 1912 and continued to be active there along with his sons Fred and Arthur until his death in 1950, aged almost eighty-eight. He had also bought the Swan Brewery in Ardwick from Chesters in 1926 and ran it with another son, Gilbert, producing vinegar. Later Chesters bought this brewery back to act as a back-up plant during the war, in case the Ardwick Brewery was bombed.

A further son, Charles Albert Hyde, succeeded him as head brewer at Chesters and soon made his own mark in the brewing ledgers by producing a new bottled beer in 1929 called Natural Ale, which sold well for more than thirty years.

But the elder Hyde's departure from Chesters coincided with an alarming drop in trade as the Depression hit Manchester hard. Sales slumped to less than 700 barrels a week in 1931. Fighting Mild lost some of its punch as gravities were reduced to cut costs and keep prices down. Its strength was further sapped by wartime restrictions after 1939.

Chesters expanded into northern Lancashire to try and boost trade, notably buying pubs in Preston. Many were home-brew houses, but the breweries were quickly closed. One, however, at the Derby Arms, carried on brewing until 1950. It was famous for its strong ale Uncle Jim.

In 1961 Chesters merged with Threlfall's of Liverpool to try and create a stronger group in the North West. The move marked the beginning of the end for the Ardwick Brewery. Charles Albert Hyde retired in 1963 and three years later the site was closed, with production moved to Threlfall's Cook Street Brewery in Salford. But despite having more than 800 pubs, Threlfall's Chesters felt it was still not big enough to survive alone and in 1967 accepted a £24 million bid from national giant Whitbread.

Most Chesters and Threlfall's beers soon disappeared, but the Best Mild refused to lie down, fighting on as one of the main beers brewed at Cook Street, though by now its gravity was just 1032 (3.5%). The Chesters name even made a major comeback in the early 1980s, with the Salford site renamed Whitbread Chesters. But this late flourish was not to last, with the towering Victorian brewery axed in 1988.

A severely weakened Fighting Mild was on the ropes and was finally knocked out at the end of the century, after a few years being brewed at Whitbread's Exchange Brewery in Sheffield and then at Everard's of Leicester. But its memory refused to die.

One of CAMRA's founders, Graham Lees, who grew up in the area, remembers it well:

> I can still smell it now as the drays delivered to the corner pubs in the streets where we played as kids. It was dark and hoppy and lip-smacking when I first got my lips around it aged about 13 at a family wedding.
>
> I think the tag 'fighting' had less to do with the strength of Chesters than the rowdy Manchester/Salford pubs, where large volumes were drunk. Mild was more popular then, pubs were busier and punch-ups ensued from the two.

ODD BUT TRUE: Chesters Brewery was closely linked with Manchester City Football Club in its early years, providing its Hyde Road ground. The formation of Ardwick AFC, as City was originally known, had taken place at Chesters' Hyde Road Hotel in 1887. Stephen Chesters Thompson was the club's first president. The association lasted until 1917.

BEER: Davenports' Beer at Home
BREWER: John Davenport & Sons, Birmingham
ALSO KNOWN FOR: Davenports' Bitter and Top Brew de Luxe
BREWERY LOGO: Malt sack with ears of barley
HISTORIC RIVAL: Ansells of Aston
SIMILAR BREWS TODAY: The historic Highgate Brewery of Walsall revived Davenports' Bitter early this century before being renamed Highgate and Davenports Brewery in 2009, such was the pull of the famous name. Beer at Home was even brought back from the dead - only for the brewery to go into liquidation in 2010 and then be rescued by a new consortium. Davenports' dramatic life continues.
ILLUSTRATIONS: 22-5, 84

BEER AT HOME: Davenports were different. 'We're an odd company,' admitted a smiling head brewer, Tony Muntzer, when I visited the Bath Row site in Birmingham in 1979. The reason was simple. It was emblazoned above the stylish columns surrounding the entrance. In large letters were the words 'Beer at Home'.

In a highly conservative industry this meant going against the grain. Even fermenting trouble. Most breweries built up a large pub estate. Davenports focused on selling beer direct to people in their homes. Years before supermarket vans roamed the streets, their smart lorries and salesmen dropped off crates of bottled beer on your doorstep.

This unusual sales strategy had been born out of necessity. The company, dating back to at least 1829 when Robert Davenport was brewing in Hockley, ran into financial and family problems after forming a limited company as John Davenport

& Sons in 1896 with fifty-seven pubs. Most of the houses had to be sold off and two of the sons split what remained of the business between them in 1904. Jack Davenport kept the Bath Row brewery, the few remaining pubs and the company name, while Baron Davenport launched a bold new venture.

According to popular legend, he disliked parents sending their children round to the local pub with a jug every time they wanted a drink at home. So he established a bottling company and set up delivery rounds. Discounts were even given to regular customers as part of a profit-sharing scheme.

Despite opposition from rival brewers and retailers in the city, this scheme was so successful that by 1929 Davenports CB & Brewery (Holdings) Ltd was formed to acquire the share capital of John Davenport & Sons. The brewing company had become a subsidiary of the Beer at Home business. It accounted for up to 80% of production.

In 1935 a book celebrating its progress boasted that Davenports had a transport fleet of 140 motor lorries, delivering 90,000 tons of beer a year to 175,000 regular customers. It claimed to have 'the most up-to-date beer bottling plant in existence', capable of producing 24,000 bottles of beer an hour. The temperature-controlled bottled beer store could hold 100,000 cases.

And the customers were not just in the Midlands. Depots were opened across the country, with the trade stretching from South Wales to London and as far north as Leeds. Flagship pubs were opened in each area, like the elegant New Inn at Hayes in Kent with its own ballroom. Or the oak-panelled Nelson at Wallasey on the Mersey. Birmingham was not neglected, with the dramatic Black Horse built at Northfield.

By 1938 Davenports was recognised as among the top five brands in the UK for drinking at home in a *John Bull* magazine survey, behind only Guinness, Bass, Whitbread and Watney. Beer at Home was so successful it also attracted a copycat rival. In 1937 a Birmingham beer war broke out in the city's suburbs, with bottles flying from both sides.

The first anonymous bottle appeared in the *Birmingham Mail* on 7 September. 'Notice the attractive shape – it will not look out of place on the table at a dinner party,' boasted the advert. 'The paper label is abolished.' Instead a coloured oval would be part of the smooth amber glass. 'You'll appreciate this bottle almost as much as the contents!'

The next day the next teaser appeared, this time for the 'specially designed and patented' wooden case for the bottles, with a built-in opener. This was followed by 'the van that brings the case that holds the bottles'. But still no mention of the brewery. Then on 10 September all was revealed.

In a full-page advert for Ansells' 'revolutionary' Home Service, the Aston brewery launched a new department. 'You'll be proud to have your beer delivered this modern way: smart covered vans; courteous uniformed drivers; neat handy cases; clean hygienic bottles – tradesman's, not drayman's, delivery.' In a dig at Davenports' profit-sharing scheme, it added, 'You'll need no special inducement to buy Ansells – the Better Beer.' The beers on offer in 'magnums' were Nut Brown, Pioneer Pale and Tonic Stout.

Then Davenports struck back on 14 October. Its advert featured a report from the 1910 AGM of Birmingham Licensing Committee in which Joseph Ansell of the Wholesale Brewers' Association 'viewed with considerable apprehension and alarm the continued prevalence of beer-hawking'. He said, 'The conduct of this particular class of business in the suburbs ... is contrary to the public interest, pernicious and objectionable.' At the time brewers felt direct deliveries threatened sales from their off-licences. Ansells owned around 300. Now it had joined the 'pernicious' beer-hawkers.

In its next large advert Davenports pointed out that, unlike Ansells customers, 205,854 people benefited from its profit-sharing scheme; the amount paid out during the past ten years adding up to £446,603. Then it let one of the trade's great secrets out of the bag.

Brewers were notoriously shy about revealing the strength of their beer. But on 28 October 1937, Davenports published the original gravity of its most popular beers: Bitter 1039; Brown Ale 1044; Best Bitter 1052 and Extra Stout 1054. 'These prices and gravities challenge comparison with those of any other brewery ... when you're told about price – ask about gravity!' It claimed to offer the best value for money in Britain and to be the only brewer publishing gravity figures.

Davenports dubbed Ansells' scheme a 'side-line service' while Beer at Home was the beating heart of its business. 'In the face of intense trade prejudice and opposition, this policy triumphed.' Ansells' competition certainly did not seem to hurt the maverick brewer. By Baron Davenport's death at the age of seventy in 1939 it had a quarter of a million customers. Ansells' assault on the doorstep market had not dented its trade.

It wasn't rival brewers but the rise of the supermarkets which undermined Beer at Home. By 1979 the once dominant deliveries only accounted for 35% of production, with the number of depots cut back from eighteen to thirteen as distant outposts were closed. Davenports focused on canning and plastic bottles for the supermarkets and in 1985 sold off Beer at Home to Hazeldown Supplies of Cannock, with the beer later brewed by Holden's of Woodsetton, near Dudley.

Davenports reverted back to being a traditional brewer, relying on its pubs. It had bought Birmingham rival Dare's with forty houses in 1961 and added a further twenty-nine when Thornley-Kelsey of Leamington Spa ceased brewing in 1969. It was a policy that seemed to be paying off. In 1978 *Sunday Mirror* readers voted Davenports Bitter the best real ale in Britain.

But becoming a traditional brewer brought traditional dangers. In 1983 Wolverhampton & Dudley Breweries bid to take control but were beaten off. They bid again, only for Greenall Whitley of Warrington to pip them with a £38 million deal in 1986. Three years later the Bath Row brewery was closed, with production of Davenports beers briefly moved to Greenall's subsidiary, Shipstone's of Nottingham. The original home of Beer at Home had delivered its last drop.

ODD BUT TRUE: At the height of the takeover drama in 1986 a bugging device was discovered taped to the underside of Davenports' boardroom table.

BEER: Double Maxim
BREWER: Vaux of Sunderland
ALSO KNOWN FOR: Samson Ale and Vaux's Stout
BREWERY LOGO: John Bull and a griffin's head
ILLUSTRATIONS: 26, 27, 85, 86

DOUBLE MAXIM: Two of the best-known beer brands in Britain are Guinness and Newcastle Brown Ale. Yet if a brutal war had not intervened and history had been kinder to one north-eastern brewing company, it might, just might, have been Vaux's Stout and Sunderland Brown Ale – also known as Double Maxim.

Sent to cover a story in the 1970s about the building of a golf course on an old rubbish dump in Darlington, I found the excavated ground littered with broken glass and hundreds of thick, green, stoppered bottles, most embossed with the words 'Vaux's Stout'. It was all that remained of a shattered dream.

Cuthbert Vaux had founded his brewery in Sunderland in 1837, eventually settling on a site in Castle Street in 1875. His grandson, also Cuthbert, pioneered bottling at the brewery in the 1890s. By the time the company produced a calendar in 1900, there was clearly only one beer to promote – Vaux's Stout.

A beaming John Bull was pictured holding up a bottle above an appreciation from the *Lancet*. 'In the brewing of this stout it is said that by paying greater attention to the operation of mashing an increased proportion of nutritive substances appears in the wort and hence in the stout,' said the medical journal. 'The results of our examination confirmed this statement.' It contained a hefty 6.55% alcohol by volume. 'The digestive action of malt has been pushed ... to a maximum degree.'

The calendar showed C Vaux and Sons Ltd, registered in 1896, had stores not only in Newcastle, Middlesbrough and Darlington, but also in Glasgow and Leeds and 'agents in all north country towns'. Letter headings said Vaux had been awarded three gold medals for its stout. Tramcars in Scotland advertised the brew. It claimed to be 'Britain's Best'. A famous poster showed a burglar with his pockets stuffed with bottles, beneath the slogan, 'Among other things, I always take Vaux's Stout.'

It was marketed as 'highly nutritious' at a time when many brewers claimed their stout 'was good for you'. Local Sunderland rival, Northern Eastern Breweries, which merged with Vaux in 1927, declared that their Malt Stout was 'strengthening and invigorating'. Customers found these dark claims difficult to resist. But there was a black cloud on the horizon – the First World War.

The Government's harsh restrictions on beer strength and production during the conflict left British stout's body painfully thin. But the rules were not enforced in rebellious Ireland. Guinness poured in to fill the gap. Already well known in England with huge trade, it could now clinch the market. Sales soared to such an extent that Guinness opened a brewery in London in 1936 to keep up with demand. The challenge of Vaux's Stout in the North faded away. Like most British breweries, it began selling Guinness.

But the Wearside company had another weapon in its arsenal. Maxim Ale was named after the Maxim machine gun, invented in 1884 by Hiram Maxim. It had first been brewed in 1901 as a strong brown ale to celebrate the return from the Boer War of Major Ernest Vaux, who had commanded a Maxim gun troop. This was more than a quarter-of-a-century before Newcastle Brown Ale was introduced in 1927. But Maxim's strength was also sapped by the First World War, and it only began firing again at full throttle in 1938. At the same time its name was changed to Double Maxim.

But the fightback came far too late. Newcastle Brown by then dominated the market and Double Maxim was always in the legendary flint bottle's shadow. The Tyneside company even dared to advertise its 'broon' as 'the one and only' in Sunderland Football Club's match-day programme.

However, Vaux was much bigger than its beer brands. By the late 1970s it was one of the largest brewing companies in Britain outside the Big Six national combines. Besides its Sunderland plant, it had two breweries in Edinburgh – Lorimer & Clark, taken over in 1946 and Thomas Usher, added in 1959. Lorimer's Scotch was a big seller in Vaux pubs in the North East. Its trading area stretched as far north as Perth (Wright's Brewery taken over in 1961) and as far west as Kendal in Cumbria (Whitwell, Mark in 1947). It had also expanded to the south, swallowing Ward's of Sheffield in 1972 and Darley's of Thorne in South Yorkshire in 1978. In addition to its 900 pubs, there was an expanding hotel division, Swallow Hotels, and a major wine and spirits business, Blayney's.

But finding a flagship beer was still a problem. It had by now nailed its future to the mast of a Viking longboat, with the launch of Norseman Lager in 1970, after the failure of keg Gold Tankard in the 1960s. The new golden hope was produced with Danish help and Vaux was developing a surprising taste for the continent. In 1974 it took over a Belgian brewer, Liefmans of Oudenaarde, noted for its strong Flanders brown ales. In 1977 it negotiated a deal with French brewer, Brasseries Semeuse of Lille, to import its premium lager Stelbräu in return for Semeuse taking Lorimer's Golden Strong Ale. It was exporting Lorimer's to Germany and importing Paderborner Brauerei's Diät Pils.

In 1981 the group's ambitions stretched across the Atlantic, when it surprised the US industry by taking over the Koch Brewery of Dunkirk in up-state New York. 'For once we are ahead of the Americans,' said marketing manager Peter Heyward. 'We shall use the brewery to meet the growing demand for high-quality beers, like the Anchor Steam Brewery has done on the West Coast.' Double Maxim was exported to Seattle and San Francisco. Vaux was going global. It even opened two pubs in Melbourne, Australia, as well as a handful in London.

Then they woke up from their dreams. The bold moves were not paying off. The US and Belgian breweries were sold in 1985, Darley's shut in 1986 and Lorimer's let go in 1987. Vaux had already closed its other Scottish plant and sold its 214 pubs north of the border to Allied Breweries in 1980. Norseman's long ship also hit the rocks in 1985 and was replaced by Tuborg. Vaux was pulling back to northern England – and finding solace in an old friend in a new form.

Double Maxim was launched on draught in 1989. Rich and nutty, it was mashed with crystal malt, a dash of caramel and primed with sugar. Only traditional Fuggles hops were used. Beer writer Roger Protz described it in 1994 as 'vastly superior' to Newcastle Brown, despite being lower in strength at 4.2%. It was also still merrily innovating, launching Britain's first wheat beer, Weizenbier, in 1988 and a honey beer called Waggle Dance in 1995.

The company had also invested in a modern German brewhouse, but as increasing numbers of breweries began to pull out of brewing, pressure began to mount in the City for Vaux to do the same and concentrate on its more profitable Swallow Hotels.

In 1998 the board caved in and agreed to quit brewing. The ruling Nicholson family had lost control and managing director Frank Nicholson's bid to buy the breweries and 350 pubs was rejected early in 1999 despite strong local support. Chairman Sir Paul Nicholson quit in protest and fans of Sunderland FC, sponsored by Vaux, gave the closure decision the red card at their next home match. Production at Vaux and Ward's of Sheffield ceased in July. Before the end of the year, the new Swallow Group was swallowed by Whitbread. 'In less than 160 days, a company with 160 years of history had committed suicide,' said Frank Nicholson.

But it was not the end of Double Maxim. Former Vaux executives Doug Trotman and Mark Anderson bought the brand and, helped by ex-head brewer Jim Murray, began brewing it again – to the strength of Newcastle Brown (4.7%). First it was produced at Robinson's Brewery in Stockport, then the beer came home to the North East in 2007 with the opening of the Double Maxim Brewery in Houghton-le-Spring.

Max was back – while Newcastle Brown was out. After the closure of its Newcastle brewery in 2004, it is now brewed at John Smith's in Tadcaster, North Yorkshire.

ODD BUT TRUE: Vaux briefly introduced Maxim Light in the 1980s as a low-alcohol bitter (0.9%). The new Double Maxim Brewery also produces a Max variation but at the other end of the scale – a heavyweight champion called Maximus (6%).

Above left: 2. Even the Queen Mother liked Young's Special. When offered a glass of wine in 1987 after she had pulled a pint in the Queen's Head in Stepney, she said, 'Never mind the Champagne. This is much better' (see page 6).

Above right: 3. Tetley's huntsman lost his soul once he left Leeds (see page 5).

Above left: 4. Alton Pale Ale label.

Above middle: 5. By the 1960s, Alton 'blue' was marketed as John Courage IPA (see pages 11–13).

Above right: 6. Allsopp's Arctic Ale label (see pages 13–15).

7. Allsopp's IPA was once a major rival to Bass (see pages 9–11).

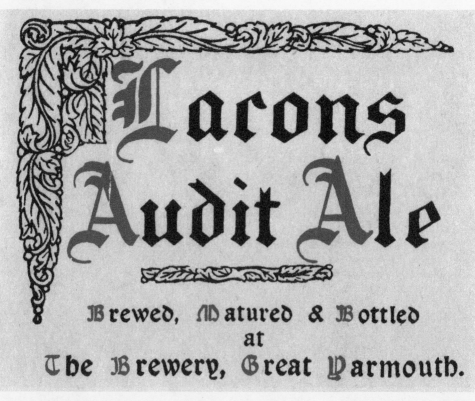

8. Lacon's Audit label (see pages 15–17).

Above left: 9. Final flourish – staff at the Dorchester Hotel in London are all smiles after receiving their cases of Audit Ale from Lacon's in 1966 (see pages 15–17).

Top right: 10. Greene King continued to brew an Audit Ale, promoting it as 'brewed from the recipe which provided the potent brew for the Cambridge colleges' Audit Feasts'.

Middle Right: 11. Barnsley Bitter became increasingly popular during the 1950s and 1960s.

12. A Barnsley Brewery poster after the company was formed in 1888 (see pages 17–19).

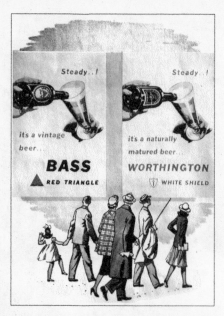

Above left: 13. Carefully does it. A barmaid pours a bottle of Bass Red Triangle – but it was little different from the Worthington White Shield on the bar.

Above right: 14. Spot the difference. Some of Bass and Worthington's marketing was becoming remarkably similar from the 1950s, apart from the label. So was the beer (see pages 20–2).

15. Further state control of pubs is ridiculed by cartoonist Moon in the *Sunday Dispatch* in the late 1940s (see pages 22–5).

Above left: 16. The ancient Queen's College brewhouse in action. The beer in the copper is being cooled off (see pages 25–6).

Above right: 17. M&B of Birmingham captured most of the market for Oxford's college ales.

Above left: 18. Morrell's of Oxford continued to brew a College Ale until its Lion Brewery shut in 1998.

Above middle: 19. For a time All Souls shared the Queen's brewery before its ale was brewed by M&B.

Above right: 20. Drinkers were urged to 'Have a Chesters with the men' in 1971 (see pages 27–9).

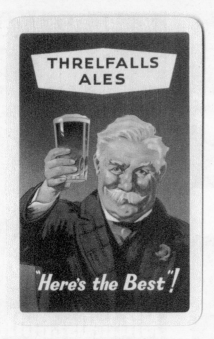

Above left: 21. Threlfall's of Liverpool merged with Chester's in 1961 (see pages 27–9).

Above right: 22. A 1952 Beer at Home advert targets busy housewives (see pages 29–32).

23. A Davenports delivery van delivering a case of beer in the 1930s (see pages 29–32).

Above left: 24. Rival Birmingham brewer Ansells came knocking on the door with its own Beer at Home service in 1937 (see pages 29–32).

Above right: 25. Customers are gently reminded to return their empties to the Davenports man.

Above left: 26. John Bull toasts the new King, George VI, in Maxim Ale in 1937 (see pages 32–4).

Above right: 27. Double Maxim was always in the shadow of the market leader, Newcastle Brown.

28. Both former head brewer Andy Hepworth, left, and managing director Bill King of King & Barnes, went on to set up their own breweries in Horsham (see pages 55–7).

Above left: 29. Once Green's took over Flower's of Stratford-on-Avon in 1954, it adopted its name and Shakespeare trade mark (see pages 53–5).

Above right: 30. Great attention was paid to marketing Dragon's Blood to fire up sales.

31. Portent of doom – King & Barnes striking boxed Millennium Ale marked the beginning of the end for the Horsham Brewery (see pages 55–7).

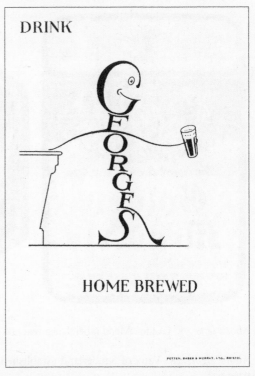

Above left: 32. Beer & Rigden were so confident that they were 'Kent's Best' they didn't always add their name to their advertising (see pages 57–9).

Above right: 33. George's used this spindly bar figure to promote Home Brewed (see pages 60–1).

Above left: 34. Fremlin's Family Ale label (see pages 57–9).

Above middle: 35. George's Home Brewed label (see pages 60–1).

Above right: 36. Breweries like Crosswell's of Cardiff adopted bees and beehives as their trademarks (see page 62).

Above left: 37. Golden Mead label. Sales reached as far as the Far East (see pages 61–3).

Above right: 38. Vaux of Sunderland established Waggle Dance as a national brand (see page 63).

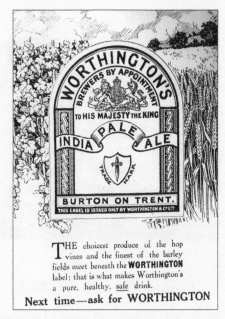

Above left: 39. Beer's healthy reputation was being shredded during the arsenic scare, as shown by this cartoon from the *Daily Dispatch* in 1900, in which the brewer tells his assistant to chuck everything in as 'I'm only a-mixin fourp'ny' (the cheapest mild) (see pages 63–6).

Above right: 40. Even more than a decade later in 1911 Worthington's was advertising its IPA as 'a pure, healthy, safe drink' (see pages 63–6).

Above left: 41. Light Amber had eclipsed the Dark by 1959 (see page 65).

Above right: 42. After the takeover, Greenall Whitley picked Groves & Whitnall's Red Rose Stout to promote (see page 66).

43. Brewers at Bentley & Shaw's Lockwood Brewery in Huddersfield would try to drive golf balls over the railway viaduct behind (see page 68).

HAMMONDS
Good Yorkshire ALES

The sign of a Good Beer!

KUB

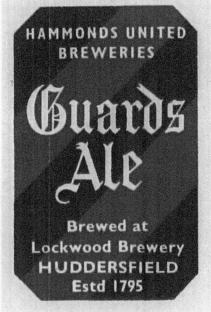

HAMMONDS UNITED BREWERIES

Guards Ale

Brewed at Lockwood Brewery HUDDERSFIELD Estd 1795

Left: 44. The Guards campaign failed to switch enough Hammonds drinkers from their usual pints of mild and bitter.

Above right: 45. Guards Ale label (see pages 66–8).

46. Guards Ale had towering ambitions – but sales fell well short (see pages 66–8).

47. Hull introduced ravens at the brewery in the 1950s – but they proved a nuisance (see page 69).

Above left: 48. On this City Ales beer mat Bill Brewer asks visitors 'Wot be gwain 'ave?' (See pages 70–2.)

Above middle: 49. Bottled Imperial was a reminder of the City Brewery's old vatted ales.

Above right: 50. Heavitree provided the only local opposition in Exeter once City and the St Anne's Well Brewery combined in 1943.

51. Workington widely used John Peel to whip up trade.

Above left: 52. Workington added a keg Golden Bitter to the John Peel pack.

Above right: 53. Slalom sent John Peel skidding into oblivion (see page 74).

54. The John Peel name was written all over the Workington Brewery (see pages 72–4).

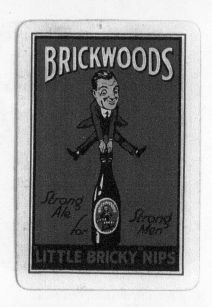

Above left: 55. Little Bricky – 'Strong Ale for Strong Men' – gave drinkers a powerful lift (see pages 76–8).

Above right: 56. Brickwood's completed its local domination of Portsmouth by taking over United in 1953.

57. Little Bricky was sold as a winter warmer in the 1950s (see pages 76–8).

Above left: 58. Mass Observation noted that Magee's brewer preferred Best Mild (see pages 78–9).

Above middle: 59. During the 1960s, men switched to drinking bitter – in pint glasses.

Above right: 60. Dutton's went one step further than Guinness and said Mercer's Meat Stout 'is better for you' (see pages 82–4).

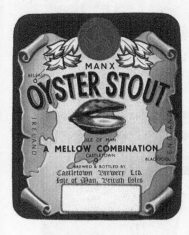

61. Guinness regularly promoted its stout with oysters, as in this 1930 advert (*right*) but Manx Oyster Stout from Castletown (*above*) actually contained oysters (see pages 80–2).

62. This feisty cockerel avoided being added to a Cock Ale by ruling the bar at the British Flag in Battersea in the 1920s (Picture: Courage Archive) (see pages 82–4).

63. Morocco Ale, brewed for Levens Hall in Cumbria to an ancient recipe, was originally said to have contained meat (see pages 82–4).

BEER: Dragon's Blood
BREWER: Flower's of Luton and Stratford-on-Avon
ALSO KNOWN FOR: Brewmaster, Poacher Brown Ale and Flower's Keg
BREWERY LOGO: Shakespeare
HISTORIC RIVAL: Whitbread Final Selection
SIMILAR BREWS TODAY: Marston's Owd Rodger from Burton-on-Trent
ILLUSTRATIONS: 29, 30, 87, 88, 90

DRAGON'S BLOOD: Few breweries have totally transformed themselves like J. W. Green of Luton. Until the Second World War the Bedfordshire brewer was little known outside its immediate area. Its best-known beer was Lutonian Pale Ale and its emblem was its initials tied in a messy knot.

Then, like a super hero stepping into a telephone box, it changed almost overnight into a dynamic, different character. And the superman with magical powers was Green's head brewer Bernard Dixon – assisted by thirsty American servicemen.

Dixon had joined the company in 1932 when the Green family ran into financial difficulties, gradually taking over the running of the firm, becoming managing director in 1940 and chairman in 1947. He had come from Greene King's Cambridge brewery after winning the Champion Challenge Cup at the Brewers' Exhibition in 1931. He was a man ahead of his time, enthusiastically pioneering the latest production techniques like enzymic malt. But US airmen made him take off in a new direction.

The thousands of Americans on local wartime airfields had little taste for 'warm' flat English draught beer. They preferred bottled beer, but bottles were in short supply. So Dixon developed a chilled, filtered, carbonated bulk beer to meet their needs. This explosive 'keg' innovation was to blow apart the traditional British brewing industry.

Dixon was also an aggressive exponent of expansion by takeover – and not just locally or regionally. In five years from 1948 to 1952 he swallowed seven breweries to create a patchwork empire of 1,000 pubs stretching from Sunderland to the south coast. Green was going national, years before the 'Big Six' brewing combines were established.

But Dixon was not just interested in beer and pubs. He also recognised the might of marketing. At a time when most brewers still sold milds, bitters and brown ales under their family name, he believed in brands. He organised elaborate conferences to ensure 'licensees and their staff never lose the opportunity of putting favourable propaganda, both about the company and its products, across the counter'.

Delegates to the fifth Annual Convention in 1954 were lectured on 'salesmanship' and how to present the new brews, with displays of bottled beers behind the bars. Above all they must keep mentioning the brand. 'It is quite an easy matter to introduce the customer to the brand name while confirming his order. For instance, the customer may order "An IPA, please" and the barman could reply "Brewmaster, sir"?'

One of Dixon's first brands had sprung out of his first major takeover, when he bought Kelsey's of Tunbridge Wells in Kent in 1948. Again he was ably assisted by American servicemen, who during the war had nicknamed Kelsey's strong ale

Dragon's Blood. Dixon liked the striking title and adopted it for his winter warmer. Everything was plotted in detail in this dragon's den, with a fiery beast drawn up to promote the brew.

Licensees had to follow strict rules. 'As soon as the customer enters one of the group's houses ... his attention will be caught by drip mats, ash trays, point-of-sale display advertising, matches and many other items.' Convention delegates were instructed to remove Dragon's Blood show-cards from the bars in late spring and display them again 'when the chilly autumn nights arrive'. Its slogan was 'The famous Old English Ale' and the dark brew lived up to its hype. Andrew Campbell in his 1956 *Book of Beer* described it as 'a strong ale that is not too sweet and that has real quality'.

But not all marketing initiatives worked as intended. At the 1957 Soho Fair a dray was to carry a huge dragon. To fire home the Dragon's Blood message, it breathed flames from its nostrils, powered by a gas bottle inside. But the dramatic display proved too hot to handle and was ruled too dangerous to use on the streets.

Other major brands included Sable Stout, promoted by the Black Knight from *Ivanhoe* under the slogan 'Liquid Luxury' and Poacher, 'The Cream of the Brown Ales'. Leading the pack was Brewmaster, 'The Master Brew' featuring a red-capped brewer on the label. A similar figure carrying a barrel was adopted as the company's logo. Green's tried hard to build an old-world image, claiming that their brewers still wore traditional red caps in the brewery. But it was an uphill struggle.

Unlike Bass the name did not mean beer to the general public. Green was too vague. For a marketing man like Dixon, it lacked impact. Then he found the solution. In 1954 the company took over Flower & Sons of Stratford-on-Avon, who were famous for their bitter and IPA, and immediately adopted their better-known name. J. W. Green became Flower's Breweries. Their Shakespearian emblem took centre stage, being adopted for a new Flower's Lager and for the relaunch of Dixon's wartime innovation – keg beer. Customers were now urged to 'Pick Flower's'. But Flower's Keg Bitter was to explode in Dixon's face and torpedo his career.

The problem was that the pressurised containers and new dispense equipment needed to serve keg beer were extremely expensive. The second problem was that this reliable beer proved surprisingly popular. Initially intended for only small free trade accounts, it was soon being demanded by the company's 1,450 tenants. At the 1957 Convention, Dixon was still urging licensees to be patient. 'I know a great many of you have strong claims for priority of supplies, but I must ask you to take my word for it that we are doing everything possible.'

And it wasn't just landlords who were becoming annoyed. The group's rapid expansion had weakened it financially, leading to cash-flow problems. At the same time costs were soaring from both the new keg beer and more ambitious marketing. In 1957 comedians Kenneth Horne and Richard Murdoch fronted TV adverts for Flower's. Large ceramic ashtrays appeared in pubs – with a bust of Shakespeare in the middle. Dixon's abrasive style also angered some of his fellow directors, and a group around the Flower family feared he planned to abandon brewing in Stratford. In 1958 they forced him out.

But with Bernard Dixon gone, the company's driving force also disappeared. After an initial trading agreement was signed with Whitbread, Sir Fordham Flower in 1962 asked the London brewer to take full control. Dragon's Blood quickly bled to death, replaced by Whitbread's Final Selection. Flower's Keg initially blossomed but then withered away in competition with Whitbread Tankard and Trophy. Only Brewmaster was fully embraced by Whitbread, becoming its export pale ale.

But the Flower's name proved much more resilient. Like a persistent weed, it kept popping up in unexpected places. The old Luton and Stratford breweries closed in the late 1960s, but the Flower's name spread west, being picked for the Whitbread Flowers division based in Cheltenham. Cask beers, notably Flower's Original and IPA, appeared in the 1980s, along with a keg Flower's Best. Bernard Dixon would have approved. Branding had beaten history again, as Flower's flourished once more on alien soil.

Even when Whitbread shut the Cheltenham plant in 1998 and then sold out to Belgian brewing giant Interbrew, Flower's refused to wilt. The beers just spread further afield, being brewed in Manchester, then Dorset and now at Brain's Brewery in Cardiff.

You can even still find Shakespeare, quill quivering in hand, waiting for a glass of Flower's Lager or Strong Ale in Italy today. The dragon may have been slain long ago, but the Bard staggers on clutching his beloved Flower's.

AS YOU LIKE IT: Charles Flower, while running the family brewery in Stratford, also devoted years to establishing the Shakespeare Memorial Theatre which opened in 1879. When it burned down in 1926, the family raised further funds to replace it. The Bard's Stratford heritage was built on beer.

BEER: Festive
BREWER: King & Barnes, Horsham, Sussex
ALSO KNOWN FOR: Sussex Bitter and Golding Ale
BREWERY LOGO: A bishop's hat (the mitre) and later just the letters K&B in a circle
HISTORIC RIVAL: Dolphin IPA from Kemp Town Brewery of Brighton
SIMILAR BREWS TODAY: Festival (5%) from Dark Star of Partridge Green, near Horsham
ILLUSTRATIONS: 28, 31, 89, 91

FESTIVE: 'The small breweries are a brotherhood. We all know each other in this part of the world,' said Tony Jenner, director of Harvey's of Lewes. 'It's funny really,' added John King, chairman of King & Barnes. 'The two of us have always been the smallest in the area, but we are the ones that have survived.'

They were talking to Fred Pearce of CAMRA's newspaper *What's Brewing* in 1978. Much bigger and much more ambitious Sussex brewers, like Tamplins and Kemp Town in Brighton or Star in Eastbourne, had been taken over and closed down, but the two minnows had escaped being hooked.

John King was in no doubt about the reason why: 'We were just determined not to be taken over; we have always enjoyed our work. Many people who did sell out must now be bitterly regretting it. I don't know any of them with bigger smiles today.'

The Horsham brewery had grown out of a maltings run by James King from 1850 in Bishopric, the cattle market of the country town. In 1906 his sons merged the business with Barnes' East Street Brewery to form King & Barnes. An estate of more than fifty pubs was built up, all within a horse-drawn dray ride. It was a small family firm focused on supplying its own houses. Only in 1975 did it venture into the free trade.

In keeping with this conservative approach, K&B stuck firmly to traditional cask beer. 'Twenty years ago we just couldn't afford to go over to keg,' admitted John King. 'Now we just smile and say we would never have dreamed of doing it.' By standing still the company had moved with the times. When the real ale revolt against keg erupted in the 1970s, King & Barnes had the right beers to satisfy campaigners.

Frank Baillie in the 1973 *Beer Drinker's Companion* was impressed by the 'very well hopped and fully flavoured' PA bitter. There was also a dark, malty XX mild and a strong XXXX old ale for winter. But hiding in the bottle store was a bigger beer.

Festive had been introduced in 1951 as a strong pale ale to mark the Festival of Britain. In 1980 it was launched on draught as the brewery's flagship strong cask bitter to mark the opening of a new £500,000 brewhouse, doubling production capacity. The original brewery was retained as well. At the same time XX and PA were renamed Sussex Mild and Bitter. The small firm was beginning to flex its muscles. With an alcoholic strength of 5%, compared to the bitter's 3.5%, Festive was a heady brew. Free trade sales soared. Later the range at the bar was broadened with Broadwood Best Bitter (4%).

By 1985 K&B's ambitions had stretched to launching its own JK Lager. Bottled beers were exported to the United States. Polypins of real ale were even flown out from nearby Gatwick airport to a bar in Hong Kong called Mad Dogs. Energetic managing director Peter King saw a bright future. 'I'm 37 now and look forward to another 28 years working here – it's a fine life because we are independent and will remain so.'

It turned out to be a poignant prediction, as in 1994 Peter King died from a heart attack at the age of forty-six. Suddenly the charismatic driving force in the brewery had gone.

Initially business continued as usual. Festive had been launched as a bottle-conditioned beer the year before, and this policy of selling real ale in glass was expanded with Old Porter (5.5%). The former barley wine Golding appeared annually as Christmas Ale (8%). A new £750,000 bottling line was installed in 1996 followed by a 'magnificent seven' new brews. King & Barnes was the leader in this growing market, even winning the contract to brew the legendary Worthington White Shield from Bass in 1998.

It certainly needed a shield, for the firm was looking vulnerable. Production was around 30,000 barrels a year, but two-thirds of that was in the highly competitive free trade or for contract brews like Bajan Lager from Banks of Barbados. Financial pressures were mounting and in 1999 the company dramatically axed its head brewer Andy Hepworth, who had developed the bottle-conditioned beers, with managing director Bill King taking over production. At the same time its free trade distribution and wines and spirits operations were sold to cut costs. Twenty staff were made redundant.

Other brewers were circling. Within weeks Shepherd Neame of Kent made a £15 million bid. Bill King urged family shareholders to reject the deal, but also called in advisers. The result was to accept a £23 million offer from Hall & Woodhouse of Blandford Forum in 2000. The Horsham brewery quickly closed, 'Sussex' Bitter now being brewed in Dorset, while Festive was dropped. The Kings had lost their crown to the despair of drinkers.

But out of the ruins sprang not one but two local breweries in 2001. The former head brewer Andy Hepworth set up the Beer Station in the town's former railway yard. Its first beer was Kid & Bard! While Bill King established his own company, WJ King, in Foundry Lane, brewing a Horsham Best Bitter and Red River Ale in similar style to K&B's Sussex and Festive. Horsham was mashing again.

ODD BUT TRUE: When King & Barnes rebuilt the brewery in the late 1970s, no expense was spared in writing the company's name across the front. It took seventy books of gold leaf to complete the huge letters.

BEER: Fremlin's County
BREWER: Fremlin's of Maidstone and Faversham in Kent
ALSO KNOWN FOR: Three Star Bitter, AK Mild and English Stock Ale
BREWERY LOGO: An elephant, originally standing on the family's coat of arms
HISTORIC RIVAL: Farmer Ale from Style & Winch of Maidstone
SIMILAR BREWS TODAY: Larkin's Best from Chiddingstone, Kent
ILLUSTRATIONS: 32, 34, 92–4

'Before the war,' grumbled the half-and-half, 'there was no bad beer: only different degrees of perfection.'

The large bitter cocked an experienced eye into his tankard, gauging the number of swallows that remained. 'This isn't a bad wallop, but not a patch on the stuff we used to get at Territorial Army camp.'

'So you were TA, too!' put in a mild, lowering his pint enough to flip his Artillery tie. 'Where did you go for camp?'

'Some little place in Kent,' replied the bitter. 'About ten miles from Maidstone.'

The deep voice of the County Ale spoke up. 'That's the answer. Kent's the home of beer. Maidstone's the home of Fremlins. And this County Ale' – he held up his glass and gazed lovingly through the amber-shaded contents – 'is a beer of real pre-war quality: strong, warm, full-flavoured.'

FREMLIN'S COUNTY: This imaginary conversation was the first of a series of post-war adverts promoting Fremlin's County Ale from Kent in the neighbouring county of Surrey. And like a lot of bar talk over a glass or two, it glossed over the facts. For while Maidstone was the home of Fremlin's, it was not the home of County Ale.

County Ale XXXXX had originally been brewed by the aptly named George Beer & Rigden of Faversham, who modestly promoted their beers under the slogan 'Kent's Best'. The number of Xs would indicate that it was, at least at first, a strong ale, though the brewery also produced a Special XXXXXX for good measure. The company had been formed in 1922 through the merger of George Beer of Canterbury with Rigden's of Faversham. The brewery premises in Court Street had been established early in the eighteenth century opposite Shepherd Neame's even older brewery, which still survives today.

Fremlin's was a very different brewing business. For many years, it did not even believe in selling beer through 'sinful' public houses. It had been set up by a devout Christian, Ralph Fremlin, in 1861, when he bought the Earl Street brewery in Maidstone. He soon sold its ten pubs. He targeted the home trade, where he believed the tonic value of his family ales could be enjoyed in moderation. Bottle labels emphasised their purity: 'Guaranteed bittered entirely with hops'.

But it proved an extensive market built on more than a hope and a prayer. With his brothers he had, by 1894, established London branches in Buckingham Palace Road, White Hart Lane in Tottenham and in Camberwell, besides eight stores from Brighton and Eastbourne to Croydon and Guildford, as well as agencies 'including the principal watering places on the south coast'. A lager plant was added by 1891 and a 'National Temperance Ale' was produced. He also ran bible classes for his employees.

He generously supported the building of local churches and was chairman of the Maidstone School Board. He was a respected community figure. When he died in 1910, the streets on the route to the cemetery were packed with people and shop windows were shuttered in black. But once he had gone to his grave, the business changed direction. The elephant lumbered into the public bar.

After Fremlin Brothers was registered in 1920, and then a public company, Fremlins Ltd, was formed in 1928, the business began to make up for lost time, taking over the pubs of Leney's of Dover and Flint's of Canterbury in 1926 and Isherwood, Foster & Stacey of Maidstone in 1929. In the late 1930s, Fremlin's ventured the other side of London, taking over Harris Browne in Barnet and Adams of Halstead in Essex.

Then after the war came the major coup. George Beer & Rigden had about 300 pubs and a prosperous trade, but the ageing directors feared being hit by death duties. They decided to sell up and in 1949 accepted Fremlin's offer. The firm's XXXXX became Fremlin's County Ale. The Maidstone brewers even adopted its 'Kent's Best' slogan.

Then came a surprising development. Breweries often close after a takeover. They rarely reopen. Fremlin's shut the Faversham plant in 1954, concentrating production at Maidstone. But they then reopened Rigden's brewery seven years later to meet growing demand. Sales of County Ale were bowling along. It was promoted as the beer to drink at county cricket matches in the South East. An analysis by the Consumers' Association in 1960 found it had an original gravity of 1044 (4.6% abv) and was the most expensive draught bitter (10.5*d* for a half) apart from Flower's Keg (11*d*) out of twenty-five reviewed by its magazine *Which?*

The *Stock Exchange Gazette* reported in 1966 that Fremlin's had 673 pubs and 175 off-licences. It was Kent's largest brewer – and a prime target. In 1968 London giant Whitbread took control. County Ale was soon dropped on draught though it continued for a while in bottle. Instead Gauntlet keg was briefly introduced. Most of Fremlin's huge range of bottled beers disappeared, though one distinctive drop, first introduced in 1905, survived.

Fremlin's Gold Top English Stock Bitter Ale, besides being a mouthful to order, was matured for a long period. This meant that nearly all the sugar was turned into alcohol, giving a beer with an original gravity of 1040–44 a surprisingly high alcohol content of 5.4%. This made the beer ideal for those who needed to watch their diet. Whitbread adopted it, promoting it as 'Britain's bitterer bottled bitter, suitable for diabetics'.

Fremlin's Pale Ale Brewery in Maidstone closed in 1972, though it was used as a depot until 2003. Faversham continued in production, producing Whitbread Trophy. But local drinkers had not forgotten the elephant and their campaign for a revival saw the launch of Fremlin's Tusker (1046) in 1979, based on the old County recipe. It was described as 'a strong, satisfying bitter with a hoppy flavour'. The heavily dry-hopped cask Trophy 'D' was renamed Fremlin's Bitter. The elephant was back on the bar.

But Tusker's charge into the pub did not last long. 'It's a shame to put a young elephant down,' said Whitbread South East managing director Roger Tatum in 1985. However, the brewery looked safe since it was receiving major investment, only for the Whitbread board to close it in 1990. Production of Fremlin's Bitter moved to Cheltenham before being dropped in 1997. The elephant had finally packed its trunk and said goodbye.

ODD BUT TRUE: The elephant's trunk originally curled under, but it was later curled upwards to present a more forward-looking approach. The elephant was everywhere. A gilded one swung on a weather vane above the Maidstone brewery, while nodding models were produced for window displays. When the Faversham brewery closed, a bottled Elephant Ale was produced, a tear falling from the sad beast's eye on the label.

BEER: George's Home Brewed
BREWER: George's of Bristol
ALSO KNOWN FOR: George's Bitter Ale and Glucose Stout
BREWERY LOGO: A grey drayhorse
HISTORIC RIVAL: Double Brown from Whitbread of London
SIMILAR BREWS TODAY: Sarah Hughes' Dark Ruby, Beacon Hotel, Sedgley, near Wolverhampton
ILLUSTRATIONS: 33, 35, 95-8

GEORGE'S HOME BREWED: George's was a brewery built on dark beers. It had been formed in 1788 in the heart of Bristol by Philip George and six merchant partners to rival the major London companies in brewing porter, though there had been a brewery on the site since at least 1702, when Sir John Hawkins brewed his own beer for the visit of Queen Anne. Prosperous slave trader Isaac Hobhouse then built up the business in the 1730s.

Philip George had wider ambitions. Within a year he was shipping porter to Cork and Waterford in Ireland and to Liverpool. Bristol porter could hold up its head in competition with the major London brews. An agent's report on the Irish trade noted in 1792 that 'people here complain of the colour being too deep, but approve of the body, which they acknowledge considerably superior to the London. Therefore they mix them to make the London better and sell it as London Porter', he added bitterly.

By 1816 the company boasted that it sold, 'Porter, Strong Beer and West India Ale of quality superior to most breweries and inferior to none in the kingdom.' George's was developing a reputation for its winter-brewed Special Old Beer, matured in huge 1,500-barrel oak vats for at least a year. By 1888, when the company was incorporated as The Bristol Brewery Georges & Co. Ltd, it claimed to be 'one of the largest brewery businesses in the West of England'.

But by the twentieth century tastes were changing. A 1908 company profile said it 'makes specialities of light bitter ales and home-brewed beer'. Home brewed might sound today like something your uncle makes in his kitchen, but it was once a popular commercial beer style, particularly widespread in the South West of England and South Wales. It was a luscious, strong brown ale or, on draught, a full-bodied mild. The title was a tribute to the beers once produced by the vanishing home-brew pubs.

But as the strength of British beer was sapped by the ravages of two world wars, many breweries ditched the style but kept the popular name, adopting it for their standard bottled brown ale. Thus Home Brewed became regarded by many as just a local term for brown ale. As Andrew Campbell said in his 1955 *Book of Beer*, 'Home Brewed is a title often given to brown ales, and will be met especially in the West Country.'

But historically it was much more than that. Campbell admitted there were 'many types of brown ale' at the time, and HB was the top of the range, the Rolls Royce of bottled mild ales. It was a double brown, a term adopted by some breweries.

There was even, between the wars, a national brand sold across the UK. Whitbread's Double Brown was launched in 1927 and heavily promoted in the 1930s as a premium bottled beer by a strange long-necked figurine. Adverts gushed that it was a beer of 'excellent gravity and nourishing' with 'a splendid full flavour' until its body was fatally wounded in the Second World War and it was replaced by the weaker Forest Brown.

But George's continued to keep the faith. Home Brewed became for a while the brewery's brand leader, its name displayed in neon lights on the side of the brewhouse alongside the floating harbour.

It also became the company's most expensive brew on handpump. A 1947 price list reveals a pint would set you back the then considerable sum of 1s 6d, compared to 1s 3d for Bristol Stout and just 11d for the bread-and-butter Mild and Bitter. In bottle only Imperial Stout was a halfpenny more.

George's Home Brewed was not a modest drink but a rich tipple, increasingly confined to bottle. In 1954 it was the company's second-best seller in glass after Bitter, accounting for nearly 17,000 barrels a year despite its high price. A standard brown ale was only introduced after the merger with Bristol United in 1956.

Such was its reputation and unique style that it survived takeover after takeover. When George's was swallowed by Courage in 1961, most of the George's brews were swept away by Courage brands. But Home Brewed remained. The shire horse on the label even kicked off the crowing Courage cockerel and cantered through successive takeovers by Imperial Tobacco, the Hanson Trust and Australian giant Elders IXL of Foster's Lager fame.

Only thirty years after the original takeover, in 1991, was bottled Home Brewed finally axed. By then it was brewed not in Bristol, but at Courage's massive plant alongside the M4 near Reading, and its original gravity had declined to 1040. But even at that strength, it was much more than a weak brown ale. The last of Britain's true double browns had died.

One George's beer lasted longer, even outliving the old Bristol Brewery run by Courage, which closed in 1999. George's light Bitter Ale (3.3%), the traditional draught session beer of the city, was then briefly brewed by Smiles of Bristol before being dropped in 2000.

ODD BUT TRUE: Bottles of George's Home Brewed were kept on the top shelf of the Farriers Arms in St Albans, the first pub CAMRA ever switched back to real ale. Landlord George Vardy used to tell visitors it was his home brew.

BEER: Golden Mead
BREWER: Hope & Anchor Breweries, Sheffield
ALSO KNOWN FOR: Jubilee Stout
BREWERY LOGO: An ancient warrior
HISTORIC RIVAL: Honeysuckle Ale from Steward & Patteson of Norwich
SIMILAR BREWS TODAY: Honey Gold (4.2%) from Cropton Brewery, North Yorkshire
ILLUSTRATIONS: 36-8, 100, 101

GOLDEN MEAD: Think of beer and you picture barrels and tankards, pubs and handpumps, barley and hops. They are all used to market the happy drop. But just occasionally there's a bee buzzing about. For instance, take a closer look at the pump clip for what was once one of Britain's best-selling bitters, Boddingtons of Manchester. There, resting on an upright cask, are two bees.

But what are they doing there? They certainly had sweet nothing to do with the original beer, since Boddingtons was traditionally one of Manchester's most bitter bitters. And it wasn't just to emphasise the 'B' in Boddies. The bees fly right back to the earliest origins of alcoholic drink. Man soon discovered that when honey was mixed with water and left to ferment, it produced an intoxicating drink.

Ale made from cereals became the everyday thirst-quencher, but mead was the drink for special occasions, the mystic wine of northern Europe. It was the custom at marriages to feast upon mead and for a merry month afterwards – hence the term honeymoon. To eke out precious supplies of honey, it was often used to sweeten ale. So honey beers, sometimes with added herbs and spices, became a familiar part of the brewer's art. Only when beer was restricted to malt and hops did these exotic flavours fade away.

But the bee retained powerful associations with beer. Brewers in areas like South Wales, where the Celtic taste for mead lingered, liked to be linked with its healthy reputation. Both David John of Pentre and Crosswell's of Cardiff featured beehives on their labels. Brakspear's of Henley-on-Thames adopted the bee as their emblem. Their steam wagon, which trundled around the country lanes of Edwardian Oxfordshire, was known as The Busy Bee. One of their bottled ales was Treble Bee.

And then a brewer slipped the magical ingredient back into beer. Carter, Milner & Bird of Sheffield specialised in distinctive bottled beers, the best-known being Jubilee Milk Stout, introduced in 1935 to celebrate the Silver Jubilee of King George V. Shortly afterwards another beer was launched from the Hope Brewery – Golden Mead Ale.

It was the work of director Eric Bird, a pale ale primed with honey in conditioning tanks. 'Its distinctive honey flavour appealed to those with a discerning palate,' recalled his son Michael. 'The honey was supplied by an apiary in Brough in the East Riding of Yorkshire. It enjoyed a limited success on the export market after the war.'

Carter, Milner & Bird had merged in 1942 with its Sheffield rivals, Tomlinson's Anchor Brewery, to form Hope & Anchor Breweries. The new company was eager to export and hoped Golden Mead would sweeten the way. It was promoted with an ancient warrior holding up a drinking horn and the slogans, 'The finest brew of the age' and, 'The original and genuine honey ale'.

The ambitious company sponsored the International Trade Club at the Festival of Britain in London and erected 'Rose & Crown' inn stands at overseas exhibitions. At the International Trade Fair in Toronto in 1950 'such was the demand for Jubilee Stout and Golden Mead that extra supplies had to be rushed by air from Sheffield', it said.

Eric Bird visited America that year to report on sales. As a test, he sampled a bottle of Golden Mead in New Orleans that had been in transit for ten weeks: 'The barman iced it and on tasting it was found to be a really delightful bottle of beer – chilled, had a lovely head and tasted like wine.'

Golden Mead became the toast of North America, with distributors like Corydon & Ohlrich of Chicago and Reiters of New York – but also spread into Mexico, the Far East and Australia, as well as Belgium and West Africa. Hope & Anchor even considered building a brewery in Canada to meet demand, but instead made a trading agreement with Canadian Breweries. In return, it started brewing Canadian's lager in Sheffield in 1953. And this brew soon became the new golden beer. It was called Carling Black Label. By the 1960s, Golden Mead was becoming just a sweet memory.

But the busy bee was not to be banished from beer forever. In 1993 bee-keeper-turned-brewer Wil Cort began brewing Enville Ale in Victorian farm buildings on the Enville Estate in Staffordshire, using an 1850 recipe for bee-keeper's ale. Based on an IPA, it is far from sweet. But the sting is in the tail, with warming honey flavours coming through in the finish.

Its success stung bigger brewers into action. Vaux of Sunderland launched Waggle Dance in 1995, named after the rhythmic swaying of bees passing on news of the nearest nectar. Fittingly, it was brewed at its subsidiary brewery, Ward's of Sheffield. The bottled brand was so successful, it was later bought by Young's of Wandsworth. London rival Fuller's made a beeline for the same market with Honey Dew, perhaps recalling the company Fuller's took over in Brentford in 1908 – William Gomm's Beehive Brewery. The bee in beer was enjoying a third honeymoon.

ODD BUT TRUE: Golden Mead was said to be popular with ladies' hairdressers, who washed clients' hair in it to give an extra shine.

Arkell's of Swindon launched its Bee's Organic Ale in 2001 – after a swarm established a nest in the brewery chimney. The bees did not produce any honey for the brewery, but the expert called in to remove them recommended a supplier.

BEER: Groves & Whitnall's Dark Amber
BREWER: Groves & Whitnall, Regent Road Brewery, Salford, Lancashire
ALSO KNOWN FOR: Red Rose Stout and 'C' Ale
BREWERY LOGO: A red rose
HISTORIC RIVAL: Chester's Extra Best Mild from Manchester
SIMILAR BREWS TODAY: Dark Mild from Boggart Hole Clough, Manchester
ILLUSTRATIONS: 39-42, 102

GROVES & WHITNALL'S DARK AMBER: The turn of the century should have been a time of celebration for Salford brewers Groves & Whitnall in 1900. Instead, it turned into a nightmare, particularly for its eminent chairman James Grimble Groves.

Perhaps an incident that summer indicated the desperate, dark days to come. The limited company had just been formed in 1899. The booming business controlled nearly 600 licensed premises and was valued at more than £1 million. The flotation was an enormous success. Head brewer Charles Hill was made a director.

The company's 1949 history recalled that on 12 August 1900, 'Whilst he was enjoying a glass of beer at the White Hart, Cheadle, Mr Whitaker, his assistant brewer, came by on horseback. The latter dismounted and chatted with Mr Hill, who insisted on standing his horse a gallon of beer, which it drank with great relish. When they parted, Mr Hill was apparently in the best of health and spirits, but shortly after arriving at his home in Whalley Range he had a seizure and died in an hour or two.'

The death proved an ill omen. The grim news broke on 23 November: 'Poisoning in Manchester'; 'Remarkable Revelations'; 'Arsenic in Beer' screamed the headlines in the *Evening Chronicle*. 'Startling effects in Salford. Almost a plague' added the *Evening News*, which revealed that doctors in the borough had been seeing a sharp rise in serious illness, paralysis and unexplained deaths since at least June.

This had led Dr Ernest Reynolds, a workhouse hospital physician, to investigate. Many sufferers were heavy drinkers and when he analysed local beers he found dangerous levels of arsenic. When he revealed his findings in the *British Medical Journal*, all hell broke loose.

Brewers at first flatly rejected the suggestion that there was anything wrong with their beer. The Manchester public analyst Charles Estcourt supported them. 'It is in the utmost degree improbable that the beer as delivered from the various breweries contains arsenic,' he said. He blamed the adulteration on unscrupulous innkeepers.

Others pointed the finger of suspicion at chemicals used to clean casks or sulphur dressings on hops to control pests. The hop growers hit back, claiming Manchester brewers added phosphoric acid to their old ales to reduce maturation time. Beer's healthy reputation was being shredded and James Grimble Groves was in the firing line.

He was not only chairman and managing director of one of the largest local brewers, he was also chairman of the regional brewers' association and the MP for South Salford. Initially, he suggested that the epidemic might have been caused by the return of soldiers from the Boer War suffering from enteric fever or the impurity of Manchester's water supply. But public health officials soon tracked down the real culprit.

They found that sugars from Bostock's of Garston in Liverpool contained arsenious oxide due to the 'exceptionally high' levels of arsenic in the sulphuric acid used to make them. J. G. Groves breathed a sigh of relief. The sugar could be destroyed, contaminated beer recalled and business, after an almighty scare, could hopefully return to normal. Drinkers had been turning to cider, whisky and wine in their droves.

But it was not to prove so simple. The dead might be buried, but they were not forgotten. Mr Groves was dragged into court cases and inquests, where Groves

& Whitnall's 'fourpenny' (mild) had been found to contain arsenic. The brew was made using 15% glucose and each barrel was also primed with half a gallon of invert sugar, both from Bostock's. Other brewers were implicated, but only pubs were prosecuted.

And the investigation intensified with the appointment of a Royal Commission in 1901. When it finally reported in 1903, it revealed another disturbing discovery. Besides contaminated sugar, it found some samples of malt had contained arsenic for years. 'There can be no doubt that a considerable proportion of beer brewed in some parts of the country before 1900 contained noteworthy quantities of arsenic, mainly derived from malt,' it concluded. This was due to gas coke used in some maltings for drying the grain. This contaminated the malt, though at a lower level than the suspect sugar.

In northern England and the Midlands a common cause of ill-health was alcoholic neuritis, which was attributed to heavy drinking. But this nerve disease was rarely found in southern England or Scotland. Medical experts now realised that what had been harming beer drinkers was not the alcohol but arsenic poisoning.

The shocking discoveries jolted the brewers into action. Much more extensive testing of beer and its ingredients was introduced. Coal replaced coke in the maltings. Many stopped using sugars. Brewers like McEwan's from Edinburgh had gained trade in Manchester advertising their beers as 'made from malt and hops only – guaranteed free from impurities'. Groves & Whitnall, at the heart of the storm, went even further, openly declaring the ingredients on labels for their bottled ales.

Dark Amber was said to be 'a naturally matured beer of the old home brewed type, rich in malt and brewed with prize Worcester hops, most nourishing and invigorating'. Light Amber was 'a bright crisp beer, naturally matured and brewed from the best Yorkshire malt and the finest Kent hops'. Both contained 'no artificial carbonation' and were 'absolutely pure' insisted the brewery.

The company recovered only to lose its leader just before the First World War. It was also a blow for the community. J. G. Groves had developed a keen interest in the area's social problems, having founded the famous Salford Lads Club in 1903.

Then came another disaster. On 22–23 December 1940, during the Manchester Blitz, the brewery was heavily bombed. Blasts destroyed the offices and parts of the plant. 'Nothing was left of that fine range of buildings ... except a great crater and a pile of debris strewn across Regent Road,' said the firm's history. Fortunately hundreds of local residents sheltering in the brewery's huge 'C' cellar escaped. Pubs were also hit, with half of the company's houses in built-up areas badly damaged or destroyed.

But Groves & Whitnall proved resilient again. Remarkably by 17 January brewing restarted, though bottling was chilling work. 'For several months in bitter weather, the men and girls of the bottling works carried on ... under the most severe conditions. About one third of them worked totally in the open air, with their only comfort the doubtful warmth of coke braziers; the remainder in roofless and windowless buildings.'

After major rebuilding, the company celebrated its diamond jubilee in 1959 with an eight-page supplement in the *Evening Chronicle*, but change was imminent. Two years later it was taken over by North West giant Greenall Whitley of Warrington and most of its beers, apart from Red Rose Stout, disappeared, with the Salford plant closing in 1972. The brewery that had battled through so much adversity had finally been fatally struck down.

ODD BUT TRUE: In 1875 when a new brewer was needed, founding partner Arthur Whitnall adopted a strategy few would consider today. He set out to taste all the brews in the area. After much sampling, he decided the beers from a small firm, Beaumont & Heathcote of Ardwick, were 'outstanding'. Their brewer Charles Hill was appointed head brewer – and introduced the popular Mild 'C' Ale in the 1890s.

BEER: Guards Ale
BREWER: Bentley & Shaw, Lockwood Brewery, Huddersfield
ALSO KNOWN FOR: Town Mild and Town Major brown ale
BREWERY LOGO: An army officer
HISTORIC RIVAL: Yorkshire Stingo
SIMILAR BREWS TODAY: Norman's Conquest from Cottage Brewing of Somerset
ILLUSTRATIONS: 43-6

GUARDS ALE: Readers of the *Stock Exchange Gazette* on 18 March 1960 were confronted by a towering figure with legs that seemed to go on for ever and a ramrod-straight back in a smart tunic. He was gazing at a glass of beer held up to the light, though his view seemed to be obstructed by his busby fur hat pulled over his eyes. A slogan alongside proclaimed 'Guards for that six-foot feeling'.

Investors and City analysts were probably puzzled, since the other advertisers in the brewing supplement were well-known names like Bass and Guinness. Guards was said to be 'Brewed by Hammonds, The Northern Brewery'. In fact it was a local brew from its subsidiary, Bentley & Shaw of Huddersfield, that had first been brewed in 1936 in honour of the brewery chairman, Lancelot Shaw Dumaresq, a former Guards officer.

Bentley & Shaw were known for their 'Town Ales', named after Huddersfield Town's winning of the FA Cup in 1922. The bottle labels were even redesigned in the team's blue and white stripes and featured the famous trophy. The brewery's best-selling beer was its dark mild, but it also had a reputation for its strong ale, Old Timothy, as well as its extensive stocks of wines and spirits. But Guards Ale only shot to attention at the bar when it made a cavalry charge for national fame and fortune in the late 1950s.

It was a time when Eddie Taylor of Canadian Breweries was shaking the British brewing industry by taking over companies to sell his Canadian lager. But it was a less well-known Canadian who was the commanding officer behind Guards. Bob Reynolds was a sales executive hired by Hammonds to bring the latest marketing techniques to the brewing industry – but he had little experience of the beer business. Unlike Bentley & Shaw.

The Lockwood Brewery had been founded in 1795 by Timothy Bentley, who was famous for developing the Yorkshire slate square system of fermentation. With his sons, he also established other breweries in Yorkshire, notably Bentley's Old Brewery in Rotherham (1820) and Bentley's Yorkshire Breweries (BYB) at Woodlesford in Leeds (1828). The family lost interest in the Huddersfield brewery and it was taken over by Hammonds of Bradford in 1944 with 192 pubs.

Reynolds decided that Hammonds should lead their advance into the free trade with Guards Ale, a strong dark barley wine with an original gravity of 1079, sold in small bottles as a winter warmer. Many in the brewery were puzzled by the choice of this expensive niche beer. But what did they know about the world of marketing? Previously, Guards had been advertised in local newspapers with cartoon soldiers exclaiming, 'Gad, Sir? A Guards, Sir!'

Reynolds wanted this prestige product to have foil labels. But his thinking was ahead of the British printing industry, so paper ones had to be used instead. It was launched in 1957 at the Alexandra Hotel in Bradford, with models dressed as 'girl guards'. But sales did not match ramped-up production, despite reciprocal trading deals with other breweries, including the Burton giant Ind Coope.

Hammonds company secretary Anthony Avis recalled, 'The bottling hall at Lockwood Brewery was filled to overflowing with full cases, and the bottling of regular lines became impossible. So every tied house was given a quota to sell, regardless of demand, and in the free trade customers were bribed and cajoled to take more than they wanted; outhouses behind pubs were to be found crammed with Guards Ale.

'The whole affair was a disaster. By Christmas 1957 Hammonds had six months of stock at Huddersfield and the brewery near enough clogged up,' he said. 'This adventure ... nearly did for Hammonds.' Reynolds was forced out in 1958, after a TV advertising campaign failed to switch on viewers. Getting rid of the vast stocks of Guards Ale took much longer, which was why it was still being promoted in 1960.

That was the year that another Canadian came knocking at the brewhouse door. Eddie Taylor combined with Hammonds and a host of other breweries to sell his lager. Guards was soon left behind in the march to promote this new golden hope – called Carling.

The brewery beneath the awe-inspiring arches of the Lockwood railway viaduct swiftly came to the end of the line, closing in 1962 after problems with its water supply from the Horse Bank Spring and the modernisation of Hammonds' Tower Brewery at Tadcaster. Guards was also dismissed from the parade ground, being replaced by Charrington's Royal Toby by 1964.

But the extensive riverside site was retained by Bass as a depot and offices into the 1990s. The setting was too grand to ignore. A 1937 brewery booklet described it as 'approached from the highroad by an avenue of trees a quarter-of-a-mile long and hemmed in by pleasant shrubberies and flower beds'. It had never been a run-of-the-mill brewery.

ODD BUT TRUE: Brewery founder Timothy Bentley was a generous supporter of local Methodism. A visiting preacher in 1907 caused a storm when he said Huddersfield's Queen Street Chapel was 'built on beer barrels and the curse of God rested on it'.

ODDER BUT TRUE: Brewers Bill Kitchen and Reg Scully would, in a break from their duties, regularly take their golf clubs to the open ground beneath the rail viaduct and, between trains, attempt to hit a ball over the towering stone structure.

BEER: Hull Mild
BREWER: Hull Brewery, East Yorkshire
ALSO KNOWN FOR: Double Anchor and Amber
BREWERY LOGO: An anchor
HISTORIC RIVAL: Moors' & Robson's Mild from Hull
SIMILAR BREWS TODAY: Traditional Mild from the Old Mill Brewery, Snaith
ILLUSTRATIONS: 47, 103-5

HULL MILD: It was like dropping through an open cellar hatch into another time zone. With a bump. I was gazing up at a new sign saying Hull Brewery. But this was 1990. Hull Brewery had been taken over by Northern Dairies in 1972 and renamed North Country Breweries. Then, in 1985, Mansfield Brewery had bought the pubs and closed the city centre brewhouse.

Only half an hour before, I had wandered down Silvester Street for a glimpse of the old buildings, still standing but now housing smart offices and shops. There were plans for a hotel on the site. Even a pub. But no plans for a Hull Brewery revival.

I ventured inside and found myself gazing at a worn but polished plaque from the past, claiming the English Street premises were the registered offices of the Hull Brewery Co. Ltd, licensed brewers, bottlers and beer dealers. Around the walls were pictures of the old brewery, its popular pubs and even more popular dray horses.

I knew I must be dreaming, for posters also proclaimed, 'It's back! Hull Brewery Mild'. No-one would launch a new brewery with a mild. Except in Hull. It was a fishing port with a dark drinking past.

The original business had been founded by John Ward in Dagger Lane in 1765, moving to its Silvester Street site just over a century later. Registered as the Hull Brewery Co. Ltd in 1888, it took over a number of rivals, building up an estate of around 200 pubs by the 1920s. It was then that the company upped anchor and sailed off in a different direction from most of the industry – a voyage that was later to land it in stormy waters.

The brewery's trade had been built on dark mild, which was ideally suited to the local water. A visitor in 1893 describes it as 'the celebrated XXX ale'. By 1912 production was almost 100,000 barrels a year, but the First World War proved a disaster, with output halved. New chairman Major Robert Ward Gleadow decided on drastic action.

He launched a radical new method of beer production. Instead of cask-conditioned beer in wooden barrels, Hull Brewery in the 1920s introduced chilled, filtered and carbonated beer delivered by road tankers into huge porcelain gravity 'jars' in the pub cellars. These glazed vessels, containing as much as 108 gallons, were made by Royal Doulton, and alone cost £108,000. With the special Thorneycroft vehicles, the outlay was considerable. Their introduction was only possible because of the huge turnover of mild in many Hull Brewery houses.

It was a massive change, years ahead of its time. Most breweries did not turn to tank beer until decades later. Only a few major companies, like Watney's in London, ventured down this risky road in the 1920s. The brewery also focused on selling its 'crystal ales' in bottle. Mild was so popular, it was unusually bottled as mild rather than brown ale. In 1949, cans were introduced for overseas markets and ships' stores, notably with Anchor Export. It was the first to can beer for Marks & Spencer's.

Yet alongside this pioneering approach, the company also clung to tradition. It took great pride in its Clydesdale horses, still used for local deliveries. Some achieved national fame. Prince was acclaimed 'Personality' of the 1970 Horse of the Year Show at Wembley. In the 1950s it had introduced three ravens at the brewery, following the old saying that 'where there are ravens, there is good beer'. Unfortunately, Mild, Bitter and Winston proved destructive, attacking vehicles and once snatching a worker's pay packet and dropping it down a drain pipe. The birds were sent flying.

By the late 1960s the company had around 240 tied outlets after taking over Hartley's of Cowick in 1957. Annual sales approached 150,000 barrels. It was a prime takeover target. In 1972 Northern Dairies swooped for £12 million, with ambitious plans to mix milk and beer. Hull Brewery was renamed North Country Breweries. Lager was introduced, first Top Score and then Hopfenperle, brewed under licence from Feldschlosschen of Switzerland. Depots were opened in distant Tamworth and Goring-on-Thames.

But the early switch to filtered tank beer came back to haunt the company. In 1979 CAMRA removed its draught beers from the *Good Beer Guide*. Local real ale drinkers had been angered by the brewery's decision to call its mild and bitter Old Tradition when they did not mature in cask. In response, it introduced a cask Riding Bitter in 1982. But Northern Foods, as it was now known, was losing its taste for beer. It had invested large sums and more money was needed to modernise the ageing brewhouse.

In 1985 it was happy to accept a substantial offer of £42 million from Mansfield Brewery. The brewery was closed and the local beers dropped, apart from Riding Bitter. Fans of the mild were left bitter. Mild, with its dark body and creamy head, had hidden depths. It might only have had an original gravity of 1032 (3% alcohol) but it had a strong following. Appropriately, the last brew was 'six square of mild' on 15 August 1985.

Its grip on local drinkers was so powerful that four years later experienced brewery director Ken Platts and innkeeper Denis Armstrong established a large forty-barrel plant in a former fish smoke-house off Hessle Road to produce the mild to the original recipe using the original yeast. They were advised by Peter Austin, who had been Hull's head brewer before leaving in 1975 to set up new breweries across the country. Now sixty-nine, he said at the opening, 'It is nice that my last job is to bring Hull Brewery back to Hull.'

Sadly, the dream was not to last, as the brewery struggled to find sales outlets. After going into receivership in 1994, it was bought by shipping company boss Dieter Ellwood, before finally closing in 2001.

ODD BUT TRUE? The brewery escaped damage in the Blitz in 1941 because it was claimed German pilots valued the 215-foot brewery chimney as a landmark on the Humber.

BEER: Imperial Ale
BREWER: Norman & Pring, Exeter, Devon
ALSO KNOWN FOR: Oatmeal Stout and Creedy Valley Cider
BREWERY LOGO: Exeter's Coat of Arms
HISTORIC RIVAL: Tan-Tivvy Ale from Starkey, Knight & Ford of Tiverton
SIMILAR BREWS TODAY: Otter Head (5.8%) from Otter Brewery, Luppitt, Devon
ILLUSTRATIONS: 48-50

IMPERIAL ALE: In the 1950s, visitors to Exeter were greeted with the question, 'Wot be gwain 'ave?' The request in the dialect of deepest Devon was posed by a bearded yokel in a smock. The pipe-smoking rustic was everywhere from beer mats to stone jars of cider.

His name was Bill Brewer and, along with 'Uncle Tom Cobley and all', he had ridden the grey mare to Widecombe Fair, according to the popular verse. The answer to his question was 'City Ales, of course!' In fact, you didn't have a lot of choice.

Norman and Pring's City Brewery in Commercial Road had taken over its local rival, the St Anne's Well Brewery in Lower North Street, in 1943. The combined company had more than forty pubs in Exeter alone. The only local competition was provided by the Heavitree Brewery.

This concentration had compensations. According to a 1959 guidebook *In The Land of Bill Brewer*, drinkers could expect a traditional welcome. 'In this great county of combe and moor, the visitor will never be far from an inn where City and St Anne's ale may be quaffed and, 99 times out of 100, it will be drawn from the wood in time-honoured fashion.'

Dating back to 1760, the City Brewery had been run by a variety of partners. John Norman, a brewer from Chard, bought an interest in 1845 and he was joined twenty years later by Walter Pring to form Norman & Pring. The partnership was turned into a limited company in 1911. The plant was initially powered by two water wheels. One continued in use until 1953.

A well, 270 feet deep, had been bored in 1849 for better brewing water and this was used for old ales even after the town supply was adopted for regular brews. The main draught beers in its 143 houses were a mild and a best bitter. Besides pale and brown ales, the bottled beers included an oatmeal stout and an Imperial strong ale sold in nips.

The City Brewery had once been known for its vatted old ales. Its cellars, running parallel with and below the level of Commercial Road, contained towering wooden vats, many of more than 300 barrels capacity, in which strong ales were matured. Imperial was a powerful reminder of this past.

The ancient vats were not removed until the 1920s, when they were replaced by smaller glass-lined steel conditioning tanks for bottled beer. As a reminder of the olden days, the overhead wooden walkway from which the vats could be inspected was left in place, now hanging alone high in the roof.

One of the company's main trading problems was keen competition from local cider makers. Demand for beer in the county was crippled by cheaper cider. According to legend, an Exeter brewer offered his soul to the devil if he would send three frosty nights in May to destroy the apple blossom.

Norman & Pring eventually decided that if cider sales were so rosy, why not venture into the orchard as well, and established its own cider mill at Crediton in 1935. Creedy Valley Cider proved a success. Bill Brewer even leant a hand, holding up a glass on the small stone jars of vintage cider introduced for the tourist trade in 1958.

Between the wars the brewery also tried to capitalise on the county's reputation for dairy products by launching Devonshire Milk Stout. 'Each pint contains the energising carbohydrates of 10oz of pure dairy milk,' boasted the brewery. Alas, the sweet stout had to be dropped after the war as the company could not compete with Whitbread's national brand Mackeson. It was an omen of the final fate of the brewery.

The St Anne's Well Brewery had grown out of a maltsters and wine and spirits business. An impressive brewhouse was built in 1878 and named after Exeter's original water supply, the St Anne's Well, once famous for its curative powers. Water was piped to the brewery from this celebrated source.

A report of the opening in the *Exeter Flying Post* of 6 March 1878 said the brewery was set up to supply 'good, sound, home-brewed beer, and also the lighter ales for which there has of late years been a great demand'. But by the time a public company was formed in 1889, it was more ambitious. Its prospectus revealed that 'the brewery's reputation has been much enhanced by the successful introduction of the St Anne's Lager Beer'. At the time few British breweries were producing lager. But the bold move failed to pay off as demand for lager was still weak.

After accepting Norman & Pring's wartime takeover in 1943, the two breweries traded separately for more than a decade. Then in 1955 London giant Whitbread bought 18,000 shares and Colonel Whitbread took a seat on the board. Rationalisation followed. Brewing ended at the older City Brewery in 1956, with production moved to St Anne's.

But there was no protection from Whitbread's reign under the group's umbrella. In 1962 Norman & Pring accepted a bid of £1.3 million. Director John Pring said the firm would retain its identity. 'We will become a subsidiary of Whitbread, but carry on as before.' His hopes were swiftly shattered. Whitbread was building a West Country empire in which there was no place for Imperial.

Six months later it bought Starkey, Knight & Ford of Tiverton and merged the two concerns. Production was concentrated at Tiverton and the St Anne's Brewery closed in 1966. Even local rival Heavitree closed its brewery in 1970 and took the bulk of its beer from Whitbread. Though brewing did not vanish forever. In 1995 the Firkin chain, known for its strong ale Dogbolter, opened a home-brew pub on part of the St Anne's site called the Fizgig & Firkin, but it only lasted a few years.

ODD BUT TRUE: The brewery played a card trick in 1955 when it launched Nap Ale featuring a nap hand of 10, Jack, Queen, King and Ace on the pale ale's bottle label. Nap stood for Norman & Pring.

BEER: John Peel Pale Ale
BREWER: Workington Brewery, Cumberland
ALSO KNOWN FOR: Barley Brown Best Mild and Old Ale
BREWERY LOGO: Huntsman John Peel
HISTORIC RIVAL: Case's Imperial Pale Ale, Barrow-in-Furness
SIMILAR BREWS TODAY: Jennings Cumberland Ale from Cockermouth
ILLUSTRATIONS: 51-4, 106

JOHN PEEL PALE ALE: Once, a striking figure stalked the fells and inns of West Cumberland with a whip in one hand and a glass in the other:

> D'ye ken John Peel with his coat so gay,
> D'ye ken John Peel at the break of day,
> D'ye ken John Peel when he's far, far away,
> With his hounds and his horn in the morning.

The famous huntsman, celebrated in song, had been adopted by the Workington Brewery to catch Lake District drinkers. His image and name was everywhere, from bottle labels and beer mats to huge signs on the sides of pubs like the Queen's Head at Distington or the Royal Oak at St Bees. Usually he was resting in a chair, whip and clay pipe on the table, pouring himself a glass of beer while gasping the words 'at last' in anticipation. And the beer was nearly always John Peel Pale Ale.

Hiring a huntsman to chase drinkers was popular in the brewing industry. Joshua Tetley of Leeds, Eldridge Pope of Dorchester and Rayment's of Hertfordshire all used a similar red-coated figure. But John Peel was different. He was local, a farmer from Ruthwaite with his own pack of hounds. He was not just local, but a local legend. After he was buried in St Kentigern's churchyard in Caldbeck in 1854, his friend John Woodcock Graves immortalised his exploits in verse, which became a popular ballad. The local brewery was eager to tap into this fame.

When Workington produced a booklet in the 1960s promoting its 130 pubs, appropriately entitled *View Halloo!*, author W. R. Bawden was entranced by the ghostly rider: 'I picture John Peel taking his hunter over a dry stone wall in hot pursuit of Ranter and Ringwood, Bellman and True and the rest of the pack – a flashing will o' the wisp of pink against a sombre November background'.

The brewery had been founded in 1792 when the Lord of the Manor, John Christian Curwen, leased land to his partners to build a brewhouse, which began trading in 1795. It was long overdue since the old market town was being transformed in the eighteenth century into a major iron smelting centre. And out of the furnaces sprang raging thirsts.

In 1839 the business was taken over by John Iredale, a brewer from Keswick, whose brother Joseph owned a brewery in Carlisle. The Iredale family formed the Workington Brewery Co. Ltd in 1891, with John Iredale's sons Peter and Thomas as directors. The firm also acquired the wine and spirit business of J. F. Hodgson, enabling it to build up 'one of the largest and most comprehensive stocks of its kind in the North of England'.

Between the wars Workington extended its Cumbrian grip by taking over two breweries in Whitehaven, notably Spencer's Old Brewery with forty pubs in 1929, as well as its local rival, Bennett's Griffin Brewery in Workington in 1939. John Peel was riding high, having been launched into the saddle to spur on sales of bottled beer in the 1930s. The company also swallowed mineral water makers Armstrong & Dickie of Dumfries.

The family still held the whip hand in the firm's management into the 1960s, by when John Peel bottled beers including Pale Ale, Old Ale, Stout and Export were sold from Westmorland to south-west Scotland. Sales of draught Workington Mild and Bitter were also rising and a keg Golden Bitter had been introduced.

Chairman John Iredale told the 1972 AGM that sales of John Peel XXX Best Bitter and Barley Brown Best Mild in 'mini-tank' form had been 'highly successful'. The John Peel Inn at Bowness had just been modernised. But the hunt was on – for John Peel.

In 1973 Maxwell Joseph's Mount Charlotte Investments swooped to buy the business. This ambitious hotel group also bid for Jennings Brewery of Cockermouth, aiming to merge the two firms and close Jennings. After a bitter 100-day battle, it was beaten off. Jennings survived. But John Peel was about to be run over by a man on skis.

Mount Charlotte saw a golden future – for lager. In 1974 Slalom Lager was launched from Workington. 'The demand has been astonishing,' said John Iredale. But the venture veered in a new direction in 1975 when Mount Charlotte sold the brewery to Blackburn's 'Lion' brewers Matthew Brown. Lion had pounced on John Peel not only for its 112 pubs but also for Slalom. It turned the Workington Brewery into the lager-only Lakeland Lager Brewery. John Peel stumbled into oblivion, as the skier shot past.

But as CAMRA grew in influence, Lion ales struggled in the real ale market. So Brown resurrected the huntsman. In 1980, it launched John Peel Special, a premium pale bitter (OG 1041), partly based on the old Pale Ale. The beer was brewed at Blackburn but conditioned in Workington.

Sadly, it was to be a troubled final gallop. For Scottish & Newcastle Breweries repeatedly tried to take over Matthew Brown. After it succeeded at the third attempt in 1987, despite determined opposition led by local MP Dale Campbell-Savours, it shut the towering Workington brewery by the river and axed John Peel.

> For the sound of his horn brought me from my bed,
> And the cry of his hounds which he oftime led,
> Peel's 'View, Halloo!' – could awaken the dead,
> Or the fox from his lair in the morning.

ODD BUT TRUE: John Peel was not the only famous figure enlisted by the firm. Workington Brewery's Demerara Rum was named after the 'father' of the American navy, Paul Jones, who in 1778 attacked the port of Whitehaven. His aim was to set fire to ships – but many of his men preferred to raid a pub instead.

BEER: Joule's Stone Ale
BREWER: John Joule and Sons, Stone, Staffordshire
ALSO KNOWN FOR: Joule's Special Bitter and Royal Ale
BREWERY LOGO: A red cross
HISTORIC RIVAL: Draught Bass
SIMILAR BREWS TODAY: A few tried to revive the legendary beers, after Bass finally stopped brewing a pale shadow of Joule's Bitter at Burton in 1978, including Bass's own museum brewery. Then in 2010, after buying exclusive rights to the name, a new Joule's Brewery was opened in nearby Market Drayton, producing Joule's Pale Ale (4.1%) to the original recipe for Special Bitter. The red cross was back on the bar.
ILLUSTRATIONS: 107, 108

JOULE'S STONE ALE: 'Some 600 people came from all over the country at their own expense last Saturday to object to Bass Charrington's closure of Joule's Brewery, claimed to be the oldest in the country, founded by monks,' reported Richard Boston in his *Boston on Beer* column in *The Guardian* in November, 1973.

'The march through Stone in Staffordshire was led in great style by the 25-piece town band, and had that same mixture of a carnival atmosphere with underlying seriousness that I have only otherwise encountered on the first Aldermaston marches. Before and after the march, large quantities of the doomed Joule's Bitter were consumed in the pubs of the town.'

More than eighty years before, Alfred Barnard wrote in his mighty work, *Noted Breweries of Great Britain and Ireland*, 'Who has not heard of Stone Ale, that ancient and wholesome beverage, whose praises have been lauded in both prose and song for nearly 150 years?' He underestimated its reputation.

Stone, like another Staffordshire town, Burton-upon-Trent, had ideal water for brewing pale ales, and had been known for its beer since the twelfth century, when monks brewed on the site later used by Joule's. An old price list claims, 'The water from the rock gives this ale in brewing the advantages of keeping in almost any climate.' It was a claim that was to be put to the test.

For behind the High Street brewery's ale stores in Newcastle Street ran the Trent and Mersey Canal to transport the beer across England. The historic Whitelocks 'luncheon bar' in Leeds still celebrates 'Joule's Stone Ale, Always in Splendid Condition' in its windows. But the barrels rolled much further than Yorkshire.

They sailed from Hull into Europe and from Liverpool to conquer the New World. Stone Ale became popular in New York. While the *San Francisco Chronicle* of 14 July 1887 commented, 'The quality of this famous old English ale ... is today the same as it was 25 years ago, and is to be found as a favourite in many of the English alehouses in town', the beer flowed as far as New Zealand and Australia, with one shipment of 400 hogsheads to Melbourne.

Founded in 1780 by innkeeper Francis Joule, but named after his son John who ran the business from 1813, the brewery had been taken over by the Harding and Parrington families from Liverpool in 1873, and built up considerable trade in the port. Joule's red cross battled with Bass's red triangle for sales. It was a fight between the sixth-oldest beer trademark and the first.

When the company, registered in 1898, issued more shares the following year, the prospectus declared that 'the ales brewed by them have acquired considerable reputation, their right to the trademark and to the title 'Stone Ale' having been established in the House of Lords in the year 1891'. It had been a long legal battle, with challenges from major organisations like the International Red Cross.

A Victorian price list recorded Stone Ale as costing as much as Joule's East India Ale, at 60/- a barrel. They were the brewery's most expensive beers apart from its AI Export, which was sold in two qualities at 66/- and 72/- a barrel. Even other breweries were happy to take Joule's beers. Groves & Whitnall of Salford sold Stone Ale as 'C' Ale. In return Joule's sold Groves' Red Rose Stout as Joule's Royal Stout.

As well as admirers around the world, Stone Ale gained cabinets full of trophies. From 1919 it won fourteen prizes at the Brewers' Exhibition, including the championship in draught beer in 1926. When Joule's won the 1957 Brewers'

Exhibition Challenge Cup for the best bottled beer, Stone Ale still boasted an original gravity of 1049, a surprisingly robust strength for a post-war beer.

The *Brewing Trade Review* reported that 'fermentation is carried out on a dropping system, using a Yorkshire stone square type yeast'. The bottled beer was filtered but not pasteurised, after being conditioned for eight to ten days. Until 1947, it had been naturally-conditioned in bottle. Despite this shining success in glass, only 10% of production was bottled. Most Joule's drinkers preferred their beer on draught. Fittingly, draught Stone Ale took the Gold Medal in its class in 1960.

When Bass took over its old rival in 1968 for its 214 pubs and threatened to shut the site, it sparked a major protest. A fledgling beer campaign even organised a funeral and, dressed as undertakers, delivered wreaths to the brewery, attracting widespread TV and press attention, including Richard Boston. The brewery still shut in 1974, but the fall of Stone Ale set CAMRA rolling.

ODD BUT TRUE: A member of the founding family, James Prescott Joule, became a celebrated scientist. His name is still used today as a measure of energy – the joule.

BEER: Little Bricky
BREWER: Brickwood's Portsmouth Brewery, Admiralty Road, Portsea, Portsmouth
ALSO KNOWN FOR: Sunshine IPA and Admiral Stout
BREWERY LOGO: A rising sun
HISTORIC RIVAL: Pompey XXXXX from Portsmouth United
SIMILAR BREWS TODAY: Blake's Heaven from the Oakleaf Brewery, Gosport
ILLUSTRATIONS: 55-7, 109, 110

LITTLE BRICKY: This powerful old ale is the nearest beer Brickwood's produced to a tot of grog (rum and water) for the many sailors in its bars. Portsmouth's history is firmly anchored in its strong links to the Royal Navy ever since King Henry VII realised the value of this south coast harbour. And when the ships sailed in so did a strong demand for beer, leading to the port developing large breweries much earlier than most towns in England. In fact, the first major plant was built on the orders of the Tudor monarch in 1492 to refresh his fighting fleet.

The industry prospered in the port, with many of the leading figures becoming mayors, aldermen and MPs. The Brickwoods came late to this party, but once they'd gate-crashed their way in, they swamped the area like an unstoppable tsunami, drowning the competition by taking over almost all their local rivals. But it was a difficult start.

Thomas Brickwood, a builder from London, came to Portsmouth to run the Cobden Arms in Arundel Street in 1849, but died within a year. His wife Fanny bought the pub and brewhouse in 1851, but died in 1854, leaving twenty-seven-year-old son Harry to battle for trade. The streets were packed with rivals, with the number of breweries in the port having just peaked at seventy-nine. Then Harry died aged thirty-four, leaving the business in trust for his sons, John and Arthur, who launched Brickwood's on the golden brick road after 1872. Within 100 years it grew from a home-brew house into one of the largest breweries in southern England.

The young brothers began buying up pubs and then in 1880 bid £43,000 for Bransbury's Hyde Park Brewery with thirty-six pubs, financing the huge purchase through loans after their bank refused to cash the cheque. Seven years later they doubled the business by buying the second largest brewery in town, Tessier's Portsmouth Brewery with seventy pubs, for £112,000, again moving production to the new site in Penny Street.

In 1891 Brickwood & Co. was registered as a limited company. Arthur died three years later, but John continued to roll the Bricky barrel forward, buying Jewell's Catherine Brewery with seventy-two pubs in 1899 for the then colossal sum of £265,000. It was said to have the best brewing water in the area. All production was switched to the new site in Admiralty Road in 1901.

It was Brickwood's third and final move, but they continued snapping up rivals including Portsmouth's oldest surviving brewery Pike, Spicer in 1911. They also absorbed its history, now claiming to have been established in 1705. After the war, they swallowed a further nine breweries in just nine years from 1925. This included expansion to the west by taking over four breweries in Southampton, as well as Blake's of Gosport in 1926 and Long's of Southsea in 1933.

The latter takeover resulted in a secret revolution at the bar. Long's beers boasted a better reputation, winning awards for their 'Gold Cup' Ale and 'First Prize' Stout, as well as being granted the Royal Warrant in 1927 for supplying the Royal Yacht. After the merger, Long's brewer S. C. Shepherdson took over as head brewer and quietly altered Brickwood's beers to Long's recipes. Production rose from 150,000 barrels a year in 1919 to more than 225,000 barrels in the 1930s.

John Brickwood had died a baronet in 1932, having climbed from a back-street boozer to the top. But his descendants remained in charge and completed local domination in 1953 when they took over their last major rival in Portsmouth and Brighton United Breweries.

The 'Sunshine Brewers', as they became known in the 1930s, now shone from Dorset to Sussex and north to London. Exports sailed as far as the USA – led by a pasteurised version of Little Bricky – and the Far East, with a £1 million expansion of the brewery in 1962. Little Bricky was heavily promoted at home as a warming winter ale, while Sunshine IPA was 'the best beer under the sun' in the company's 675 pubs.

But the sun was about to set. Brickwood's had been linked to London brewers Whitbread since 1959 and in 1971 the national giant took the final step. The company that had taken over so many breweries was now swallowed by a bigger fish in the sea. And the trading name and brands built up brick by brick over the decades were dismantled, with the brewery finally closing in 1983.

But the names of many Portsmouth breweries live on in the elaborate tile-work decorating the fronts of many pubs in areas like Southsea. 'Brickwood's Brilliant Ales and Stouts' still shine in the sunshine decades after they were last brewed.

ODD BUT TRUE: Famous actress Helena Bonham Carter is descended from leading eighteenth-century Portsmouth brewer William Pike. A Bonham Carter sat on the Brickwood's board into the 1950s.

BEER: Magee's Mild
BREWER: Magee Marshall, Bolton
ALSO KNOWN FOR: Oatmeal Stout and Crown Ale
BREWERY LOGO: A man pouring a glass of beer from a jug
HISTORIC RIVAL: Walker's Mild from Warrington
SIMILAR BREWS TODAY: Brewer's Dark (3.5%) from Lees Brewery of Middleton Junction, Manchester
ILLUSTRATIONS: 58, 59, 111

MAGEE'S MILD: It's easy to forget, in the golden age of the lager lout and binge-drinking, to what extent mild once dominated the bars of Britain. The *Brewers' Journal* estimated that in the 1930s mild accounted for three-quarters of all beer brewed in Britain. It's also almost impossible to recall how carefully drinkers once sipped their glass of beer. There's only one way to find out – travel back in time.

Only one organisation can push open the cracked etched-glass door and peer into the bare public bar of a distant age. Mass Observation compiled a report on *The Pub and The People* in the late 1930s by sending anonymous observers into back-street locals to record what went on in this alien environment (alien to much of the middle class). It was as if they were studying the lifestyle of some exotic foreign tribe. Only this jungle was made up of the pubs in Bolton, Lancashire.

They recorded every last, ludicrous detail. One noted that in nine vaults (public bars) fifty-five men were wearing flat caps, compared to three trilbies and one bowler hat. Few were bare-headed, even indoors. While in the more upmarket lounges, hats and ties were more prominent, rather than caps and scarves.

Other statistics were more down to earth, disturbing the sawdust on the floor. One table revealed that the less seats in a bar, the more spittoons. But spitting in public was by then dribbling out, as cigarettes replaced chewing tobacco. Always prepared to provide phlegmatic evidence, one dedicated observer spent his Saturday night recording what went into one spittoon. His finding: eighteen fag ends to seventeen spits.

And what were these topers of the tap room drinking? Their choice was nearly always mild at 5d a pint or best mild, which was a penny more. Most of this was supplied by Magee Marshall, the dominant town brewer, founded by innkeeper David Magee in 1866 before merging with local rival Daniel Marshall in 1885. Best mild was described by the observers as 'nicer than the common mild'. It was 'light in colour, like bitter, which is seldom drunk here'. The ordinary mild was dark.

They noted, on a visit to Magee's Crown Brewery in Cricket Street, that the brewer preferred to drink best mild. Landlords generally estimated that 90% of their trade was in the two milds. The brewery even made sure loyal drinkers could enjoy Magee's milds on holiday by buying and building pubs in coastal resorts like Southport.

Magee's also produced an IPA at 7*d* a pint. Unusually, to compete with Draught Bass, this had once been brewed with water tankered in by rail from Burton-on-Trent into the brewery's own siding. It seemed to have been a wasted effort, as it had a doubtful reputation. The observers said, 'It isn't drunk very much except in a few pubs, is considered to be very intoxicating and to give you a bad hangover.'

Surprisingly, Bolton's thirsty working men were not knocking back pints. The common unit of drink was a 'gill', the local term for a half-pint. In the depressed years of the 1930s, when every penny counted, drinking pints was going out of fashion as fast as spitting into spittoons. On average men drank five or six gills a day (no more than three pints) – at a rate of one every 9.7 minutes according to an observer's stopwatch!

Nor were they propping up the bar all day. Hard-up drinkers rarely went out before 8.30–9 p.m. Closing time was 10 p.m. Pubs were yawningly empty at lunchtime (little food) and in the early evening. Drunks were rare except on a Saturday night.

Yet, despite people's poverty, the pub was still the centre of the immediate community. Few wandered further than 300 yards to find their local in the tight narrow streets. It was the heart of their social life, and not just for flat-capped domino players. Women did not enter the male preserve of the vault, but there was a labyrinth of other rooms. They sat in the lounge with their husbands and potted aspidistras at weekends, and enjoyed each other's company in the female preserve of the parlour during the week.

Like Ena Sharples in *Coronation Street*, they preferred bottled beer, usually stout. In Bolton their favourite tipple was Magee's Oatmeal Stout. Show-cards in the bars described it as 'thoroughly sound and well brewed from the finest quality malt, hops and oatmeal. Free from acidity and guaranteed pure'.

But for the men, Magee's Mild was best. Even after the company was taken over by Greenall Whitley of Warrington in 1958, the brewery continued to trade under its own name, before closing in 1970.

ODD BUT TRUE: Magee Marshall liked to boast that they were Burton brewers, even though they had only brewed in Britain's brewing capital for two years after briefly leasing Bell's Brewery in 1902. As late as the 1950s, large signs across the stands at Wigan's Central Park rugby league ground still declared that Magee Marshall were 'brewers in Wigan, Bolton and Burton'. Magee's had taken over Robinson's Wigan Brewery in 1894, though this had also soon shut.

BEER: Manx Oyster Stout
BREWER: Castletown Brewery, Castletown, Isle of Man
ALSO KNOWN FOR: Castletown Bitter and Liqueur Barley Wine
BREWERY LOGO: A castle
HISTORIC RIVAL: Victory Oyster Stout from Young's of Portsmouth
SIMILAR BREWS TODAY: Bushy's Oyster Stout
ILLUSTRATIONS: 61, 112

MANX OYSTER STOUT:

So, after all, there was a division on the address in Queen Victoria's first Parliament – 509 to 20. I then left the House at 10 o'clock … the tumult and excitement unprecedented. I dined or rather supped at the Carlton with a large party of the flower of our side off oysters, Guinness and broiled bones, and got to bed at half past 12. Thus ended the most remarkable day hitherto of my life.

So wrote excited new MP Benjamin Disraeli in a letter to his sister in 1837. One hundred years later Guinness reproduced the letter in an advert and were to repeat the flamboyant politician's words regularly in promotions. Guinness, like Disraeli, believed stout and oysters slipped down rather well together. The Irish brewer had used the tasty double act in an early colour advert in 1930 and tried to prise open extra sales in the USA during the decade, with cartoon shellfish shown dancing round a smiling glass.

But matching the dry taste of stout with the silky smoothness of oysters was not just for the upper class or export markets. Until over-fishing destroyed the beds, oysters were a cheap food in London, sold from street stalls like jellied eels, and enjoyed by everyone with a glass of porter. The Whistling Oyster off Drury Lane whistled up Reid's Stout to help sell its shellfish, while the Colchester Brewing Company brewed an Oyster Feast Stout to celebrate the annual oyster harvest on the River Colne. The Hull Brewery advertised its Double Stout as the perfect accompaniment for a plateful.

But then a few daring brewers took the next step – and actually started adding oysters to their beer. Though, oddly, they didn't come from local oyster beds. In fact, the stimulus seems to have sprung from the other side of the globe.

An oyster concentrate was made in New Zealand from introduced English oysters (70 dozen to the gallon) and then advertised as an approved adjunct in brewing. Ground shells had in the past been used as finings to help clear beer and, being highly alkaline, could counteract sourness. But this time the flesh was used. Adverts in industry journals in the 1930s said the concentrate improved head retention 'without a trace of fishiness'.

But some brewers sniffed greater possibilities than just longer-lasting foam – a market for an oyster stout. Hammerton's of Stockwell in London in 1938 tested adding varying amounts of the oyster concentrate to their popular Oatmeal Stout at the priming stage. Brewer Harold Read told Mike Ripley of the Brewers' Society, 'The product found favour with my colleagues and the directors, and a marketing try-out was planned. However the second or third trial consignment of the concentrate contained a faulty can which had gone bad. The smell of this was so appalling that we cancelled everything.'

But other brewers refused to turn their noses up at the idea. Young's of Portsmouth took the remaining cans of concentrate from Hammerton's and in 1939 produced a bottled Victory Brand Oyster Stout. The label proclaimed, 'Pure concentrated New Zealand oyster extract used' and 'equivalent to one oyster in every bottle'. This brew surfaced again for a few years after the war.

Another coastal brewer pursued the elusive pearl for longer. Castletown Brewery on the Isle of Man had been taken over by export brewers, Hope & Anchor of Sheffield, in 1947. H&A were known for their specialist stouts, notably Jubilee Milk Stout and Vitamin Stout, and they saw a global market for an oyster stout. And the enterprising company believed one coming from a charming harbour brewery on a tourist isle in the Irish Sea would have wider appeal than a bottle from industrial South Yorkshire.

In 1948 Castletown launched Manx Oyster Stout, aimed at drinkers abroad with the slogan 'A pearl of a drink'. Its label emphasised the brewery's location between Ireland and England. You could almost smell the sea. The smooth dark brew had oyster extract added in the copper. A consultant told the H&A board that the stout had the best chance of success in North America 'owing to the interest created by the fact that it contained oyster'. Fearing competition, directors felt they needed to move quickly. A new bottling plant was installed at Castletown in 1949 to remove a bottleneck in production.

General manager, M. R. Liversidge, then set off around the world in a bid to drum up sales. He missed Castletown's 1951 AGM because he was on an extended tour of Australia, Canada and the United States. A replica 'Manx cottage' trade stand was used at exhibitions from Toronto to New York and Los Angeles. And the globe-trotting paid off. By 1952, Castletown was responsible for 7.5% of all beer exported from Britain into the USA. More than a fifth of stout exports were Manx Oyster. By 1953, Castletown claimed to be the sixth-largest exporter in the British brewing industry.

But despite developing a cult following in California, it was an expensive exercise, as shipping from the island was a constant headache. The company even took to the air to get over the problem. The Californian magazine *Fortnight* congratulated the brewery in 1952 on 'the first known use of air freight for commercial transport of any malt beverage from the British Isles'. But the flights were also high in cost.

Hope & Anchor's early hopes of a profitable brand ebbed away, and the firm focused on selling Jubilee Stout and then Carling Lager from Sheffield. Castletown became a backwater in its plans. After H&A merged with Hammond's United Breweries of Bradford in 1960, later becoming part of the giant Bass Charrington group, its stake in Castletown was sold off by Bass in 1986 to island rivals Okell's – who promptly shut the brewery. By then Oyster Stout had long been buried at sea.

But the shellfish's stout allure refused to go away. Marston's of Burton brewed an Oyster Stout from 1995, but it proved an illusion. It contained no oysters. Murphy's of Cork developed a genuine drop with Whitbread the following year, using the liquid from 100 Galway oysters in each barrel of beer, but the cask stout proved short-lived.

In 1999 Ventnor Brewery on the Isle of Wight, encouraged by brewing consultant Fred Martin who had once worked for Castletown, not only boiled whole oysters in the copper but also added them to the fermenting vessel. 'To see what effect they had we brewed a stout without them and one with,' said head brewer Xavier Baker. 'The ordinary stout was much harsher, while the Oyster Stout was silky smooth. The oysters made a big difference.' Sales of the 4.5% bottled brew took off once *The Sun* claimed it was 'liquid black viagra', but the brewery couldn't keep it up and closed in 2009.

However, long before then Oyster Stout had returned to its historic island home. A new Manx brewery, Bushy's of Mount Murray, produced a taste of the past in 1995, using fresh oysters in the late stage of the boil. It's still a seasonal brew (4.2%) today. Other breweries have also leaped into the beds, including Mersea Island of Essex with Island Oyster (5%), Arbor Ales of Bristol (4.6%) and Porterhouse of Dublin (4.8%).

ODD BUT TRUE: The Front Street brewpub in Santa Cruz, California, used to offer drinkers a fresh experience by selling porter containing a whole oyster. It called it an Oyster Shooter as the shellfish often shot out of the glass when tilted.

BEER: Mercer's Meat Stout
BREWER: Mercer's Plough Brewery, Adlington, Lancashire
ALSO KNOWN FOR: Little else
BREWERY LOGO: Letters JM on a red seal
SIMILAR BREWS TODAY? In the mid-1990s, the Daleside Brewery of Harrogate revived the spiced Morocco Ale (5.5%), which was brewed at the Elizabethan Levens Hall in Cumbria until 1877. The recipe of this 'strong, dark and mysterious ale', which was originally said to be matured for twenty-one years, is a closely guarded secret. However, it is believed meat was once an ingredient.
ILLUSTRATIONS: 60, 62, 63, 113

MERCER'S MEAT STOUT: The British Empire was said to be built on beef and beer. When John Mercer decided to mix the two in a glass, it proved a winning combination – though it cost the small brewery its independence. The meaty brew built up such a tasty reputation, that the hungry Blackburn giant, Dutton's, swooped to swallow it in 1929.

Dutton's regarded it as a major bottled brand to be sold with slick slogans alongside its strong ale OBJ. Packs of promotional playing cards even tried to trump Guinness. 'Mercer's Meat Stout is Better for You' – one step above the Irish stout's famous line 'Guinness is Good for You'. 'When in Doubt, Take Meat Stout' added Mercer's beer mats in the bar.

The bottle label also played the health trick, boasting that MMS was a 'nourishing stout brewed with the addition of specially prepared meat extract. Recommended for invalids. Refreshing and invigorating'. A back label took the wholesome message further. It didn't quite claim to be able to raise the dead, but it certainly believed it could put life into the living: 'Mercer's Meat Stout is specially brewed for purity, nutrition and health ... tests amply demonstrate its unsurpassed value as a body builder and brain food.' Anyone with any doubts could visit the brewery's office 'where the analysis and numerous unsolicited testimonials are open for inspection'.

But what exactly was the meat in Mercer's? Dutton's was so anxious to find out when it took over the brewery, on 28 March 1929 for £81,814, that within days it had a detailed account of the materials and brewing processes drawn up. The five-page document makes fascinating reading.

The key ingredient was 'meat extract caramel'. One hundredweight and 92lbs were used in the mash tun, along with five malts, flaked maize and other sugars, to make eighty barrels of a 1056 gravity beer (about 5.5% alcohol). A further 45lbs were added in the fermenting vessel.

The extract was supplied by caramel specialists Boake, Roberts & Co. of Stratford, London. The meaty name might just describe the dark sugar's character, but Keith Thomas of Brewlab at the University of Sunderland believes it was probably an actual meat extract 'like dripping' as claimed on the label.

Meat is historically no stranger to beer. And it wasn't just an extract. Special brews like Cock Ale were made by adding a boiled and crushed cockerel in a sack to a cask of ale along with fruit and spices for a week to ten days. Highly-flavoured ingredients were used by some brewers to dispose of waste beer, masking the sourness. But others were works of rich culinary art.

The London and Country Brewer of 1742 records a recipe for the misleadingly named Egg Ale:

Take to 12 gallons of strong ale, eight pounds of lean beef cut into little bits and half stewed with a little water. When it is cold, let the gravy be put into the vessel of ale, the fat being blown off. Then let the beef with 12 eggs, their shells being only bruised but the films not broken, a pound of raisins of the sun stoned, two nutmegs, a little mace and ginger and two oranges cut round, be put into a linen bag, and hang it in the barrel before it is done working. Put in also two quarts of Malaga Sack [fortified wine] and stop it up. Let it stand for three weeks, then bottle it and into every bottle put a clove and a lump of sugar.

Such exotic – and expensive – concoctions tended to be the preserve of private brewhouses belonging to large country mansions. But the odd rat or pigeon, regular inhabitants of old commercial brewhouses, also occasionally slipped into open fermenting vessels to add a little extra body to the beer.

Mercer's Meat Stout would certainly have been salty, as 3lbs were added to the liquor (brewing water), 7lbs in the mash tun and a further pound in the copper. This would have emphasised the beer's beefy body and been welcomed by manual labourers after a long, sweaty day. It would also ensure their thirst for another glass.

Dutton's soon moved production to their Blackburn brewery, with Mercer's Plough Brewery in Market Street closing in 1936. But after the Second World War the stricter rules on advertising clamped down on the brand's extravagant boasts. And just as brewers were obliged to pour the word 'milk' from their milk stout labels in the late 1940s, so Dutton's had to drop the read 'meat' from Mercer's name. It became just Mercer's Stout.

The labels still stated it was 'refreshing and invigorating' and one beer mat in 1952 even cheekily claimed that Mercer's Stout 'really does put beef into you'. But without its meaty image, sales slipped and it was chopped.

Today the emphasis is on putting beer into beef rather than the other way round. No traditional pub menu seems complete without a steak and ale pie, while beer is regularly poured into sausages. In Newcastle, butchers George Payne of Gosforth make a black ham cured with Tar Bar'l Stout from the Allendale Brewery of Northumberland.

ODD BUT TRUE: Charlie Bamforth, the Professor of Malting and Brewing Sciences at the University of California, once received an e-mail from a woman asking if the difference between Guinness brewed in Dublin and that in London was that they marinate a dead cow in the Irish version. He replied, 'I have never heard anything quite so stupid. Everybody knows it to be a dead sheep.' He fears he may have started the latest urban myth.

BEER: Meux's Porter
BREWER: Meux & Co, Horse Shoe Brewery, Tottenham Court Road, London
ALSO KNOWN FOR: Imperial London Stout and Treble Gold
BREWERY LOGO: A horseshoe
HISTORIC RIVAL: Reid's Porter from the Griffin Brewery, London
SIMILAR BREWS TODAY: Meantime London Porter (6.5%)
ILLUSTRATIONS: 114, 166-8

MEUX'S PORTER: London has suffered many disasters, but none was more bizarre than the one which hit the heart of the capital on 17 October 1814 – when eight people were killed by a destructive wave of dark beer.

Storehouse clerk George Crick told the inquest how the terrible tragedy happened:

> I was on the platform about 30 feet from the vat when it burst. I heard the crash as it went off and immediately ran to the storehouse where the vat was situated. I found myself up to the knees in beer. The vat which had given way had been full of beer within four inches. It contained 3,555 barrels.
>
> The first object I saw was my brother; one of the men had just pulled him out from among the butts. Another man, who had been working at my brother's side, was brought out in the same situation – they are both in a dangerous way.
>
> The whole vat we found had given way, as completely as if a quart pot had been turned up on the table. A brick wall of the brewhouse was blown down,

which was 22 inches thick in the strongest part and 25 feet high. It had knocked over four butts and staved several – the pressure was so excessive. The houses next Russell Street and New Street were much damaged, but I do not know the persons who were buried in the ruins. The body of Anne Saville was found on our premises. We discovered her about an hour and a half after the accident. She was then quite dead.

Crick had feared the ten-year-old vat might be suspect. 'An hour before the accident a hoop was started; hoops frequently burst,' he said. 'I spoke to Mr Young, one of the partners, about a hoop flying off. He is himself a vat builder and he said no harm whatever would ensue ... Mr Young told me to write to his father, that the hoop might be mended. Soon after I had written the note, the accident took place.'

Altogether 'between eight and nine thousand barrels of porter have been lost' the clerk added, as a neighbouring vat had also been breached. The beer in the vat which had exploded had been nine to ten months old. The sour stench stayed in the surrounding streets for weeks.

The fatal accident had not just sprung out of complacency – but also overweening pride. The major London porter brewers were among the richest men in the country and liked to compete with each other to build the most impressive storage vats. These giant vessels did not just provide a more stable environment for maturing beer, they were also mighty monuments to their owners' commercial and social standing, attracting eminent visitors to their premises.

Sir Henry Meux, a cousin of Lord Brougham, had been a partner in the Griffin Brewery in Liquorpond Street (now Clerkenwell Road), but left after a bitter feud with partner Andrew Reid and in 1809 bought the Horse Shoe Brewery, founded in 1764.

His father Sir Richard Meux had previously built the largest vat in London at the Griffin Brewery. *The Times* in 1795 reported that 'its size exceeds all credibility, being designed to hold 20,000 barrels (720,000 gallons) of porter'. It had cost 'upwards of £10,000'. A previous vessel holding half that amount had measured 60 feet across and 200 people had dined inside with an equal number standing to toast Mr Meux's achievement.

Henry Meux had similar grand ambitions at the Horse Shoe Brewery, where a visitor in 1812 said the largest vat contained 18,000 barrels. Another held 16,000. You can almost sense the Meux family swelling with pride – and the pressure mounting on the rivets. Something was bound to burst. Some members of the Meux family were declared insane. It was fortunate that it was only one of the smaller vats that collapsed.

What followed was also a monument to business values of the time. All those who had died had been women and children living in neighbouring slum tenements. Some were trapped while at a wake for a young child in a cellar. The inquest concluded that they had met their deaths 'accidentally and by misfortune'. But the brewery focused on petitioning Parliament for a rebate on the duty paid on the lost beer. They succeeded and received the huge sum of £7,300. The families of the deceased relied on collections.

At least the disaster seems to have ended the mania for building ever larger vats, though declining porter sales may have been a more significant factor. Drinkers were switching to mild and pale ales. Meux was the last London brewery devoted entirely to porter, only starting to brew ales in 1872. A few years later, according to *Old and New London,* the brewery housed just eight vats, compared to seventy in 1812. The largest held 1500 barrels with the others 900 to 1,000. Vast vessels were in the past.

Its business was restricted by its prime site at the Oxford Street end of Tottenham Court Road. Its brewery was also dated. Chairman William Harris bluntly told an EGM in 1906, 'Our site is not only far too valuable for stabling horses and washing casks, but our brewery is so badly planned and constructed as to render economic production impossible'. He was eager to cash in and move out.

Eventually, Meux bought Thorne Brothers brewery at Nine Elms in 1914 and moved production there in 1921. They also adopted Thorne's Treble Gold as their premium pale ale. The dark ages were fading away, though a thin porter was still brewed between the wars with a weakened original gravity of around 1037. It was a shadow of its former self, while actors haunted its old haunt. The Dominion Theatre had been built on the original Horse Shoe Brewery site.

Meux merged with Friary, Holroyd and Healy of Guildford to form Friary Meux in 1956, before being swallowed by Allied Breweries in 1963. The Nine Elms brewery was turned into an Ind Coope depot. Only a few years before a Night Cap Stout had been introduced as a sweet reminder of the old porter days. Now they were laid to rest for good, though Allied resurrected the Friary Meux name during the 1980s.

ODD BUT TRUE: Lady Meux (1852–1910), a former barmaid at the Horse Shoe Tavern next to the brewery, spent £20,000 on six guns to defend Ladysmith during the Boer War. Later she left most of her fortune to the admiral who commanded the battery – on condition that he changed his name to Meux.

BEER: Nimmo's XXXX
BREWER: John Nimmo and Son, Castle Eden, Co. Durham
ALSO KNOWN FOR: Castle Eden Ale and Nimmo's Export
BREWERY LOGO: The family's coat of arms and later a red star
ILLUSTRATIONS: 115-17, 169

NIMMO'S XXXX: The stained posters looked as it they were from the 1950s. A hand held out a golden glass above the words 'Nimmo's XXXX, the liquid legend returns'. But this was 1999 and the man relaunching the beer was football legend Jack Charlton. One of England's World Cup heroes, he had been chosen because

1966 was the last time XXXX had been brewed. Now the famous drop had returned after thirty-three years to mark the saving of the County Durham brewery from closure. But it was to be an all-too-brief moment back in the spotlight – for the beer and its charming country brewery.

Farmer John Nimmo had taken over the Castle Inn with its small brewhouse in 1826 and gradually expanded its trade, later helped by his son William. The old coaching inn closed in the 1850s to allow development. By the 1870s the brewery was known for its 'celebrated' stout as well as mild, pale and Scotch ales, produced in extensive premises behind the former inn's elegant façade, with a clock above the archway.

It may have been near a local beauty spot, Castle Eden Dene, but there were many mines in the area providing thirsty customers. When a limited company was formed in 1892, it had forty-five pubs mainly in the coalfield villages. Five were called the Colliery Inn.

But it was no backwoods business. Whitbread archivist Nick Redman in his official history said, 'Extensive alterations completed in 1910 made Castle Eden one of the most up-to-date breweries in the country.' Output almost doubled between 1906 and 1914, helped by building hotels and taking over Chilton's Brewery in Seaham Harbour in 1912 with a dozen pubs.

The First World War not only brought this expansion to an end, but proved a body blow to the family when the chairman's only son, William Leslie Nimmo, was killed in action in 1918, aged nineteen. After a brief post-war boom when production hit 42,000 barrels a year, trade slumped in the 1920s and was slow to recover. The main growth was in bottled beer and by the Second World War this was approaching a third of output.

Chairman William John Nimmo soldiered on through another conflict before celebrating his eightieth birthday at the Grand Hotel in West Hartlepool in 1949. He died aged eighty-two in 1952 having spent sixty-two years with the brewery. He had attended the limited company's first board meeting in 1893. His last board meeting in 1952 was just days before his death. It was a remarkable record. And almost as remarkable in a male-dominated industry, his eldest daughter Eileen Trechman now took the chair. Two sons-in-law, John Booth and Charles Macfarlane, became joint managing directors and, despite a woman being in charge, XXXX was still marketed as 'brewed for men'.

She presided over a surge in sales with draught beer more than doubling from 32,000 barrels in 1948 to 72,000 in 1963, as the company's red star shone in the free trade helped by the purchase of twelve pubs in Sunderland in 1954 and twenty pubs on Tyneside in 1958. The country brewers were moving into the major towns. And the move called for a change in emphasis at the bar.

Nimmo's ales were down-to-earth miners' beers, the best-selling draught beer by far being known as 'Ordinary'. Many pubs only stocked the basic brew, alongside bottled Star Pale Ale, Brown Ale, Stout and Export. But when Bill Doig became head brewer in 1948, he determined to promote the better quality brews, notably Nimmo's XXXX. It was a distinctive beer. As the number of Xs indicate, it was not a best bitter but a strong golden mild, bottled as Gold Brew Extra Ale with the slogan 'tops the lot'.

It was just part of a fresh approach. Nimmo Grills were introduced in some pubs and beer canning equipment was installed in 1957. A Glen Eden whisky was launched in 1959. You could drink Nimmo's Gin with Nimmo's Tonic. There was even a Schloss Lager. But as merger mania started to sweep through the industry, Nimmo's looked for a safe haven, after becoming a public company in 1956. The prime aim of the board was to keep the brewery open and it settled on the Whitbread group in 1963, after Mrs Trechman obtained a pledge from Colonel Whitbread to keep the plant in production 'for at least the next five years'. In fact, it was to last a further thirty-eight years.

At first XXXX gained extra momentum, as it was put into the ninety-two Flower's pubs around Sunderland controlled by Whitbread. But the Nimmo's name and beers were soon stripped away from its own 125 pubs as Whitbread brands took over, notably Trophy. In 1966 Castle Eden began to brew Mackeson. In 1970 Brew 70, 'the new big taste of the 70s from Whitbread' was launched from the site – and quickly crashed into oblivion.

But though part of Whitbread East Pennines, the brewery was sufficiently far from London to develop a strong local identity, now under the Castle Eden name. Beers like Best Scotch, Castle Keep and Castle Eden Ale, introduced in 1978 and using the Nimmo's coat of arms on its pump clip, had a distinct Durham flavour. Most were primed with sugar because North East drinkers like a touch of sweetness. In fact Castle Eden Ale became a national real ale, with 25,000 barrels sold a year. Head brewer Lance Ogden turned into a TV star, as he fronted the adverts.

Under general manager Jim Kerr, the brewery became Whitbread's cask beer centre after winning a group competition to brew a revival of Whitbread's Porter in 1992. Brews included Winter Royal and Fuggles Imperial. It was a major transformation since 1977, when Castle Eden's real ale sales were down to six outlets for cask Trophy. Then Whitbread pulled the plug and announced early in 1998 that the brewery was to close.

Normally that's the end. Full stop. But a minor miracle followed. The North East revolted against the London decision. Clubs threatened to boycott Whitbread beers. Drinkers, unions and councils protested. Local MP (and new Prime Minister) Tony Blair backed the battle and businessmen bid for the brewery. Whitbread backed down and sold the brewery, along with the vital clubs brand Trophy Special, to partners David Soley and David Beecroft, supported by Jim Kerr. John Constable's local craft Butterknowle Brewery also moved production to Castle Eden.

And Nimmo's XXXX rose from the dead to celebrate. A former brewer, Roger Booth, had kept the original recipe, which included flaked maize. As the 4.4% brew used no coloured malts, it was as pale as Pilsner with a soft malty sweetness balanced by spicy Goldings hops. The golden oldie was back to haunt the bars once more.

The problem was keeping the mash tuns full after the loss of so many Whitbread beers. It was an uphill struggle. Castle Eden even began brewing Chinese lagers for the South China Brewing Company, while trying to build up a pub estate. But after Jim Kerr left in 2000, David Soley announced that he was in talks to buy the threatened Cameron's Brewery eight miles away in Hartlepool – and the deal would be funded by developing the Castle Eden site for housing. The brewery that escaped Whitbread's axe was finally chopped in December 2001. Castle Eden had been sacrificed to save Cameron's.

Nimmo's XXXX kissed goodbye to home and moved to Hartlepool, but the ghostly brew was always in the shadow of Cameron's mighty Strongarm and today is little more than an occasional brew.

ODD BUT TRUE: During the First World War, the Northumberland Hussars were stationed at the brewery for more than a month. Squadron orders included the following: 'Any person failing to stop or attempting to escape when challenged by a sentry or patrol is to be shot. Discretion must of course be used in the case of inebriated persons.'

BEER: Oakhill Stout
BREWER: Oakhill Brewery, Oakhill, Somerset
ALSO KNOWN FOR: Old beer and porter
BREWERY LOGO: A horse-drawn covered wagon
HISTORIC RIVAL: Reid's Stout from London
SIMILAR BREWS TODAY: Hook Norton Double Stout from Oxfordshire
ILLUSTRATION: 118

OAKHILL STOUT: 'Guinness is Good for You' is still a memorable slogan, shining out of the dark glass years after advertising standards officers ruled it out of order. The Dublin brewer used the line in its very first press promotion in Britain in 1929.

Some brewers went further, claiming that their rich, warming stouts could almost revive the dead. Barrett's Brewery of Vauxhall in London produced a poster in 1896 showing a seriously ill woman, miraculously restored to health, proclaiming that Barrett's Stout 'saved my life'. Physicians often prescribed stout as a restorative for their patients. For this reason many extra or double stouts became known as invalid stouts – and none were more celebrated than Oakhill.

A small village in the Mendip Hills near Shepton Mallet, Oakhill seems an unlikely place to find a famous brewery. But the site was chosen because of its local springs. The water proved ideal for brewing stout and what had begun as a small venture, founded in 1767 by two Somerset gentlemen, Jordan and Billingsley, gradually expanded.

A visitor to Oakhill around 1910 recalled the sprawling enterprise which had taken over the hamlet: 'On entering the village the large malt houses on the right compel attention, and almost immediately afterwards the brewery is reached. Here we see no lordly pile of architecture, but rather an unassuming structure of irregular dimensions, which has apparently grown and grown in spite of itself, until its octopus-like extensions have covered a very large area, the extent of which can only be appreciated by progress through the interior.'

Inside the visitor would have been impressed by row after row of large vats where the stout was matured. Some were so large that when a public company was formed in 1889, a candlelit celebration dinner was held in one 500-barrel vessel.

By the turn of the century the brewery had an output of 2,000 to 2,500 barrels a week. The trade in the West Country, Wales and the West Midlands, with further agencies in Manchester and London, was so extensive that traction engines moving the barrels in and out of the brewery wore ruts in the road in places two feet deep.

The damage to the country roads was so bad that the district council complained, compelling the company in 1904 to build its own private railway line running two-and-a-half miles from Oakhill to link up with the Somerset & Dorset Railway at Binegar. The narrow-gauge railway operated two small locomotives called Oakhill and Mendip to push and pull the heavily-laden trucks up and down the steep gradient.

The brewery produced three qualities of cheaper pale ale, plus two old ales and a brown stout, but its flagship brew was its mighty mouthful Double Stout Invalid Porter (as it was described in an early price list). This was the only beer initially bottled. It claimed to have been 'pre-eminent' since 1767. 'Imitation and "just as good" brands only prove the merit of the original.'

The brewery was in no doubt about its distinction, producing a booklet in 1910 praising its recuperative powers. 'It is scarcely possible to over-estimate the value of a beverage for which it can be truthfully claimed that it is not merely a thirst quencher, a stimulant or a pleasing adjunct to the daily dietary ... but it is of the utmost value to all who are in any way debilitated, run down or in weak health.'

The Oakhill Brewery backed up this claim with impressive references. The medical publication, *The Lancet*, praised it as 'a really nourishing stout'. Its analysis showed its alcohol by volume was 7.48%. It described it as 'sound yet ripe' being 'mild to the palate, free from acidity, and does not contain an excess of carbonic acid gas'.

Oakhill's reputation soared – and so did sales. The 1910 booklet proclaimed, 'For 140 years this celebrated stout has been sold practically upon its merits alone, and yet so potent has been the reputation it has acquired, that the consumption has steadily increased all through this long period, more especially during the past 25 years, during which time the demand has increased by leaps and bounds.'

Little did the brewery know what catastrophes lay ahead. Four years later came the First World War and with it draconian government restrictions on malting and brewing. Strong English stouts like Oakhill were virtually wiped out, as the strength of beer was drastically reduced to conserve grain, while power restrictions prevented dark malts being made. The trade was left wide open for a certain Irish brewer to mop up.

A second catastrophe hit Oakhill as it struggled to recover from the ravages of war. On 16 January 1925 a fire swept through the brewery, destroying not only most of the plant but also all its records and recipes. The heat was so great that it melted the wax on the deeds in the safe and fused them together.

The brewery never brewed again. Within a few months the Oakhill company had been sold to Bristol United Breweries, which just used the site as a depot. Though BUB brewed an 'Oakhill' stout, it never regained its pre-war reputation. Only the maltings up the road remained in operation, later run by Courage. Oakhill's slogans 'Fresh from the breezy Mendips' and 'One of England's purest products' had vanished in smoke. Guinness had never had it so good.

But brewing in Oakhill did not disappear forever. In 1981 the old walls of the brewery echoed once more to the sound of rolling barrels, when a former brewer with Higson's of Liverpool, Gerry Watts, started the Beacon Brewery. The venture soon folded, but local farmer Reg Keevil had been impressed by the possibilities and in 1984 established the Old Brewery, Oakhill, on the site, later simply known as the Oakhill Brewery.

In 1997, it moved to a larger site in the former maltings, producing a strong roasted stout called Black Magic Special to celebrate the move. The old invalid had briefly risen from its death bed, and was relaunched in bottle as Oakhill Original in 2001. But it was not to last long. When Mr Keevil retired in 2004, Oakhill Brewery closed again.

ODD BUT TRUE: In the 1925 fire which destroyed the brewery, all the workers' wage packets were engulfed as well. But not everything was lost. Staff spent the next days sieving the ashes to retrieve half-crown coins, florins and sixpences.

BEER: OBJ (Oh Be Joyful)
BREWER: Dutton's, Blackburn, Lancashire
ALSO KNOWN FOR: Special Bitter and Mercer's Meat Stout (see separate entry)
BREWERY LOGO: The letters OBJ forming a cartoon figure
HISTORIC RIVALS: Old Dan and Big Ben from local rival Thwaites of Blackburn
SIMILAR BREWS TODAY: Thwaites revived a rich, dark OBJ (6.5%) in 2010
ILLUSTRATIONS: 119, 170, 171

OBJ: One of my earliest memories of beer – though I didn't know it at the time – was a strange man perched on the side of the Fox and Grapes near my home in Pudsey, near Leeds. He had a large round head, a big body and one crooked leg. He was admiring something in his hand, but it was the happy smile on his face that struck me as a child. It was only later that I connected the two – the glass and the grin. He was smiling at a goblet of Dutton's OBJ.

The House of Dutton, as the company liked to be known, had deep foundations. It dated back to 1799, after the Vicar of Blackburn leased land to farmer Thomas Dutton and his son William to build a brewery. OBJ was said to be just as old. Its parchment-style bottle labels proclaimed that Oh Be Joyful was 'a genuine Old English Ale brewed since 1799'. But OBJ was not its original name.

When the company published a book in 1949 to mark its 150th anniversary, it revealed:

Of the different ales brewed by Dutton's, Old Ben is made by exactly the same process as it was in 1799, and is a really strong old English ale. It is on record that once a year 52 barrels of this particular ale were delivered to Lovely Hall in Clayton-le-Dale, a supply that lasted the household for 12 months. This ale had a very high gravity, but it is satisfactory to know that, despite wars and government restrictions, Old Ben is still more than four-fifths as strong as it was 30 years ago [in 1919].

But the author admitted, 'Modern tastes demand bottled beer, consequently Old Ben is bottled under the name of Oh Be Joyful or, as it is commonly known, OBJ.' The title came from the infantryman's popular name for beer during the First World War – a drop of Oh Be Joyful – when they were delighted to get a drink. OBJ continued the military tradition by bringing a smile to soldiers' faces during the Second World War, as Dutton's exported 'considerable quantities' to troops in the Far East.

The dark, well-hopped brew, which had originally been stored for six weeks after racking, was promoted as 'mellow and rich' and was still being brewed to an original gravity of 1061 (around 6% alcohol) during the 1960s. By then it was all bottled as OBJ except at Christmas, when Old Ben was sold on draught. A little Old Ben was also blended with Dutton's thin dark mild (1030) to create a stronger Best Mild (1037) for a few pubs.

Brewer Peter Ratcliffe recalled, 'When Old Ben was being racked, there was, strangely, a very high incidence of drips from overhead beer pipes, necessitating buckets being put underneath.' These buckets kept disappearing. 'The head brewer Tony Wallis once challenged a man carrying a half-full bucket. He answered: "I'm doing some whitewashing, sir, and I always put some Old Ben in to help it stick better." Tony replied: "Really? Good man, then carry on." It was a legendary escape!'

The smiling OBJ figure became the company's prominent emblem, not only on bottle labels and beer mats, but on the outside of its growing number of pubs stretching from the Lake District to the Yorkshire coast after buying the Kirkstall Brewery in Leeds in 1936. 'OBJ1' even featured on the number plate of the managing director's Rolls Royce. Dutton's barrel was on a roll, continuing to take over rival breweries, including two in 1959 – Crown of Bury in Lancashire and Glasson's of Penrith in Cumbria.

But three years earlier the Blackburn business had made a fatal connection, when it became an associate company of Whitbread. In 1964 the London brewing giant swallowed Dutton's and its 784 pubs, with most of its beers soon disappearing to be replaced by Whitbread brews. Though the combine did adopt Dutton's tank beer brand – Trophy – for its standard bitter across the UK.

Whitbread West Pennines briefly revived the local name in the early 1980s with a Dutton's Bitter, but it did not last long. But it proved more difficult to wipe OBJ's smile off the face of the earth. It had such a loyal following that Whitbread continued to brew OBJ as a 'strong brown ale' with a reduced gravity of 1049–1055 (around 5% alcohol) well into the late 1980s. This was long after it had closed the Blackburn town centre brewery in 1978, after opening a modern plant at Samlesbury near the M6.

ODD BUT TRUE: In 1963 a young entertainer released a song called 'Oh Be Joyful' on Piccadilly Records, which Dutton's promoted on beer mats. His name?

Bruce Forsyth. It was strange timing, as that was the year that another OBJ, brewed in the opposite corner of England, suddenly vanished.

BEER: OBJ (Oh Be Joyful)
BREWER: Beasley's, Plumstead, London SE18
ALSO KNOWN FOR: Arsenal Extra Stout and Beasley's Dark Brown
BREWERY LOGO: Invicta, the White Horse of Kent
HISTORIC RIVAL: Barclay's No. 1 Southwarke Ale
SIMILAR BREWS TODAY: Brakspear of Witney, Oxfordshire, celebrate Christmas with a dark fruity draught beer called Oh Be Joyful (4.8%).
ILLUSTRATION: 172

OBJ: Plumstead was once a quiet rural area, where hops were grown, when Davis's 'steam brewery' was established on Cage Farm in 1845, encouraged by the quality of the well water from the underlying chalk. In 1871 the North Kent Brewery was taken over by Mitchell, Beasley and Phillips, with Charles Beasley becoming the dominant figure, building a bigger brewery in 1888. But just as the London suburbs roared out to swamp the village, so the London brewer Courage rolled out to crush Beasley's in 1963. The brewery was closed within two years and another OBJ was no longer joyful.

Beasley's had built up trade not only for its standard milds and bitters – 'Brown or Pale, Best of Ale' was one of its catchy slogans – but also for its range of stouts, including an Imperial Stout. But its flagship beer was an extra strong ale, OBJ, marketed as 'the beer for a cold day' and sold in distinctive small black bottles.

When Beasley's produced a complimentary guide in 1932, its author could barely keep his hand steady as he wrote about 'a really famous beer, that wonderful OBJ'. He gushed, 'We must not lose sight of that unique product of the firm and one in which they take great pride. We refer to OBJ'. The letters stood for O [no 'h'] Be Joyful. 'In cold weather OBJ reigns supreme as a really warming beverage and it has often been referred to as port wine ... while not a few consider it an unfailing cure for influenza.'

It was rated so highly that when Beasley's built a towering bottling store in 1931, OBJ stood out in huge letters on the walls of this local landmark. It included a cold store at almost freezing point 'with cold air circulating day and night' containing more than 50,000 gallons of maturing beer in glass-lined steel storage tanks.

Beasley's might have been much smaller than Dutton's, but it had a high profile. It was a venture favoured by royalty from Queen Victoria to King George V. The company received its first Royal Warrant in 1874, probably due to the strong military connections of nearby Woolwich, and this honour of being brewers to the Royal Family continued through three monarchs down to 1936.

But when Courage came calling in 1963 for its seventy-five pubs and nineteen off-licences, this rich liquid heritage was poured away. OBJ and the other Beasley beers were discontinued, apart briefly from Treble Star Pale Ale.

ODD BUT TRUE: A Beasley's pub, the Old Mill on Plumstead Common, was built around the base of an old windmill. It's still pulling pints today.

BEER: Old Ram
BREWER: Thomas Ramsden and Son, Stone Trough Brewery, Halifax
ALSO KNOWN FOR: Best Mild and Stone Trough Ale
BREWERY LOGO: A large letter R in an octagon
HISTORIC RIVAL: Webster's Old Tom
SIMILAR BREWS TODAY: Ram Tam from Timothy Taylor of Keighley
ILLUSTRATIONS: 120, 121, 173, 174

OLD RAM: They used to loom out of the dark, hackles raised, crowing for all they were worth. Huge, blue, neon cockerels glowing on the front of pubs with the words 'Cock o' the North' across their proud chests. To a sleepy child sat in the back of a car on the way home from visiting relatives in Halifax, the startling signs for Whitaker's Shire Ales were a little frightening.

Others were more comic. Webster's pubs had a bizarre fat figure outside, brandishing something above his head while clutching a mug. He looked like a tortoise standing unsteadily upright on his back legs – and about to fall over.

But another sign was plain puzzling. Some pubs around the Pennines had boards advertising Ramsden's Stone Trough Ales. Didn't they provide glasses? I imagined thirsty drinkers dunking their heads into long troughs of beer.

The three breweries dominated their home town. Whitaker's XXXX kissed the spot for many. Webster's were known for their light mild, Green Label Best. Ramsden's were also famous for their milds, light and dark. But it was a stronger brew which butted the brewery to national prominence.

In 1932 Ramsden's Old Ram won the 50-guinea Challenge Cup for the best bottled beer at the Brewers' Exhibition in London, after topping its class for non-deposit beers with a gravity of 1046–60. The prestigious victory meant reporters from the sponsors, the *Brewing Trade Review*, came from the capital by train to discover the secrets of their success.

'Halifax is an unexpected place. One comes on it suddenly after having given up all hope of ever arriving. No two guards or porters will ever agree as to whether a passenger should change at Wakefield, Bradford or not at all,' they reported. 'We arrived at Halifax and we had already visited Hull.'

After their trials and tribulations, they found the family brewery relaxed and welcoming. 'Surnames appear to be irrelevant at Ramsden's, either as regards directors, brewers or employees.' They were impressed by the striking buildings built by renowned brewery architect William Bradford in 1890 'in the heyday of his powers' – and by the prime location.

It lies in a commanding position in the centre of the town, overlooking the wide square, or circle, from which many streets emerge. Advantage of this position is taken by a large illuminated sky sign above the brewery offices, from which are radiated messages of cheer in broad and kindly Yorkshire: 'Tha'll Noan Ail wi' Gooid Ale, if it's Ramsden's' and 'Best Ale i' t' Shire'.

They found its success lay in 'the soundness of the system of brewing and the up-to-date nature of the plant'. Surprisingly, the Stone Trough Brewery had abandoned the Yorkshire stone square system of fermentation. 'The stone – or rather slate – squares have been scrapped and replaced by copper fermenting vessels ... brought into line with old practice by frequent pumping and circulation of the fermenting wort.'

Another reason for its victory was the yeast. It was so highly regarded within the industry that 'a constant supply' was sent to a brewery in Burton 'and to several other breweries'. The cool cellars were 'excavated from the solid rock'.

The 'naturally matured' beer for bottling was not rushed. It was kept in tin-lined copper tanks for two to three weeks for conditioning and then chilled and cold stored for a further ten days before being filtered and bottled. It was not carbonated or fined.

The visitors were entertained by former Elland MP and chairman George Ramsden and left much happier than they arrived. 'In fact, we came away – some hours after luncheon, be it noted – fully convinced that our cup had been worthily won.'

Ramsden's tried to spread Old Ram's glory to its better-selling beers by producing a display card for its pubs showing 'The Stonetrough Family' of 'naturally bright sparkling fellows' walking away with the Challenge Cup, with humanised bottles of Stone Trough (mild), Riding Ale (bitter) and Double Stout striding out with Old Ram.

Old Ram's success gave it a head start over Webster's popular Old Tom and Whitaker's powerful Bantam (1070), a little battler in a nip-size bottle. Whitaker's also brewed a weaker Old Tom (1040) for sale on draught in winter. But Old Ram never ventured far from home. When Ramsden's supplied brand details to the *Brewery Manual* in 1953, it described the strong ale as 'sold within 30 miles radius of Halifax'.

After the war Ramsden's tried to round up its local rivals, after buying the small Spen Valley Brewery of Cleckheaton in 1951. For there was a major problem with the brewery's prime site in the centre of town – no room for expansion. The Ram was cornered.

In 1958 Ramsden's had to arrange for Webster's to carry out some of its bottling. At the end of the decade, it tried to form Halifax United Breweries with Webster's and Whitaker's to compete with the growing brewing groups. But the talks broke down.

Instead in 1964 it merged with Tetley's of Leeds, part of Allied Breweries. By then it owned more than 200 pubs. But while Old Ram was soon put out to pasture once the Commercial Street brewery closed in 1967, Ramsden's Best Mild lived on for many years, brewed at Tetley's. Later it was called Tetley Pale Mild and then Falstaff Best.

ODD BUT TRUE: Ramsden's Stone Trough Brewery was demolished in 1969 to make way for the Halifax Building Society's new head office.

BEER: Plymouth Heavy
BREWER: Plymouth Breweries, Stonehouse, Plymouth
ALSO KNOWN FOR: No. 1 IPA or Devon Pale Ale
BREWERY LOGO: Entwined letters PB or an anchor
HISTORIC RIVAL: Tivvy from Starkey, Knight & Ford of Tiverton
SIMILAR BREWS TODAY: Brain's Dark from Cardiff
ILLUSTRATIONS: 122, 123, 175-7

PLYMOUTH HEAVY: Scottish sailors must have been delighted to find 'Heavy' on sale in the bars of Plymouth. For Heavy was the popular term in Glasgow and Edinburgh for a standard pale ale. When a pint was pulled their delight turned to dismay – for instead of a light-coloured brew, they were presented with a beer as black as sin. Welcome to Plymouth Heavy, a mild with a misty past.

Even Frank Clayton, head brewer for thirty years, admitted in 1980 he did not know how the name weighed in. It's hardly surprising since Heavy was not originally a PB brew. It flowed from another Plymouth brewery, the Tamar, taken over by Simonds of Reading in 1919. This brewery, near Devonport Dockyard, was famous for its dark beers, while Plymouth's Regent Brewery in Stonehouse was better known for its bitters, though it did also brew an Anchor Stout and a sweet Brown Imperial Stout.

Plymouth Breweries had been formed in 1889 by the merger of five local breweries, with production concentrated at the Regent Brewery. After Simonds merged with Courage in 1960, and Plymouth Breweries with its 235 pubs was taken over ten years later for £6.5 million, the local rivals were part of the same group. Courage ceased production at the Tamar Brewery by 1975, with Heavy finding a new home at the Regent. It had once been a heavyweight brand, but was now a pale shadow of its former self.

Brewery worker Jack Shapter, who moved with the beer, told beer writer Roger Protz, 'Heavy used to be the number one seller at Tamar. They brewed a porter too – I can remember when that was 6d a pint in 1936. But in the 1940s and 50s Heavy was the main beer, the working man's beer. Affluence created the move towards bitter beer.'

He believed the beer had been named Heavy to compete with 'Tivvy' from rival Devon brewers Starkey, Knight & Ford of Tiverton. Simonds had, he claimed, hoped to confuse customers into buying their beer. Known as Tamar Heavy, it was brewed for Devon and Cornwall only, costing 1s 1d a pint in public bars in 1953.

But by the late 1970s sales of Heavy were down to 40 to 50 barrels a week. At such a low level most breweries, particularly those in a national combine, would have ruled the beer not viable and ceased production. But the Plymouth brewery was different.

64. When Martin Sykes revived his family's Selby Brewery in 1972, it was the first new independent brewing company in Britain for fifty years (see page 7).

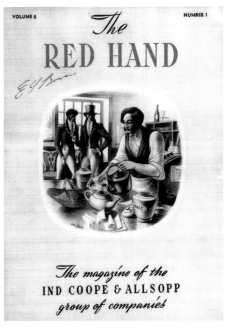

Above left: 65. Allsopp's IPA was supposed to have first been tested in a teapot, as fancifully illustrated on the cover of the company's house magazine in 1952.

Above right: 66. Allsopp's switch from IPA to promoting lager abroad did not pay off (see pages 9–11).

67. Allsopp's grand brewery in Burton-on-Trent, built in 1859, was one of the marvels of the age (see pages 9–11).

Above left: 68. Bass soon overtook Allsopp's to dominate the pale ale trade.

Above right: 69. Courage portrayed a rustic view of the past in their promotion of Alton Pale Ale (see pages 11–13).

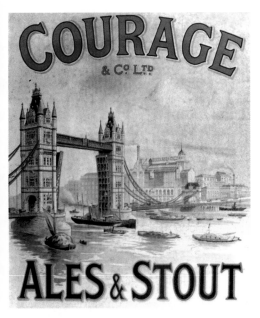

Above left: 70. Before buying the Alton brewery, Courage had pale ales shipped up the Thames from Fremlins in Kent to its brewery near Tower Bridge.

Above right: 71. Like Bass, bottled Alton IPA was sold in red (naturally matured) and blue (filtered) forms (see pages 11–13).

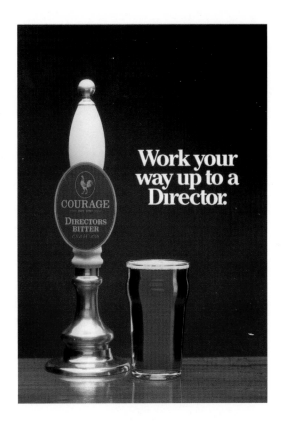

72. Alton IPA later appeared on draught as Courage Directors.

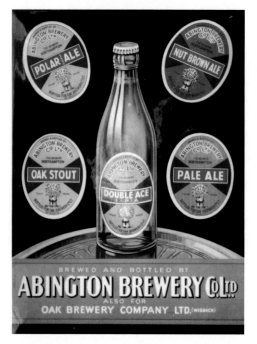

Above left: 73. Abington Brewery of Northampton tried to jump on the Arctic dog sledge in the 1950s with its Polar Ale (top left).

Above right: 74. Ind Coope launched a major promotion of Arctic Ale in the early 1950s as the beer that 'keeps out the cold' (see pages 13–15).

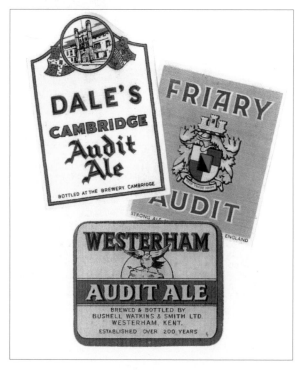

75. Local Cambridge brewer Dale's also brewed an Audit Ale, as did Friary of Guildford and Westerham of Kent (see pages 15–17).

Above left and right: 76 & 77. Barnsley Bitter is still brewed today by Acorn and Oakwell breweries (see pages 17–19).

78. Bass increased its advertising in the early 1950s to counter rising Worthington sales (see pages 20–22).

79. Worthington's sales surged after the Second World War (see pages 20–2).

Above left: 80. Bass poster.

Above right: 81. Beer was severely rationed and many pubs were shut in Carlisle during the First World War, as lamented by this postcard (see 22–5).

Above left: 82. Carlisle bottle label (see pages 22–5).

Above right: 83. Mitchells & Butlers of Birmingham already brewed a warming Old Ale (see pages 25–6).

84. Ansells of Aston liked to claim their ales were 'The Better Beer' (see pages 30–2).

85. A 1909 poster promotes Vaux's Stout and Maxim Ale as 'Britain's Best' (see pages 32–4).

86. Vaux tried to sail ahead with Norseman Lager in the 1970s, but failed to plunder sufficient sales.

Above left: 87. Dixon did not highlight Green's name on the Dragon's Blood label (see pages 53–5).

Above middle: 88. Left standing – Brewmaster pale ale survived the takeover by Whitbread (see page 55).

Above right: 89. Despite being called a strong light ale, Festive was rich, fruity and reddish in colour (see pages 55–7).

 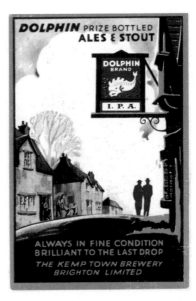

Above left: 90. Dragon's Blood was replaced by Whitbread's Final Selection following the takeover, as shown on this tray. Flower's Keg only lasted a few years (see page 55).

Above right: 91. Larger Sussex brewers like Kemp Town of Brighton and its 'Dolphin Ales' had disappeared into the sunset in the 1950s (see pages 55 and 57).

Above left: 92. County Ale tried to bowl over cricket fans (see pages 57–9).

Above middle: 93. In the 1960s Fremlin's grand elephant became a comic character.

Above right: 94. Whitbread continued to brew Fremlin's English Ale for diabetics (see page 59).

95. George's Bristol porter brewery in 1788 was soon challenging the London brewers for the market in Ireland (see page 60).

Above left: 96. Many other West Country breweries like Usher's of Wiltshire produced a Home Brewed (see pages 60–1).

Above right: 97. Whitbread's rival Double Brown was promoted by a long-necked bottled gentleman (see pages 60–1).

98. The name Home Brewed was used widely across South West England (see pages 60–1).

THE CREAM OF MANCHESTER.

Boddingtons Draught Bitter. Brewed at the Strangeways Brewery since 1778.

99. A sharp slice of Manchester's heritage disappeared when Boddington's brewery shut (see page 6).

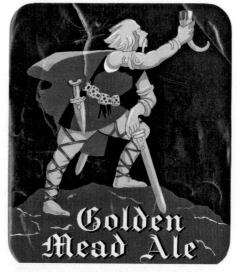

Above left: 100. The Enville Brewery put the bee back into beer (see page 63).

Above right: 101. An ancient warrior was used to promote Hope & Anchor's Golden Mead Ale to emphasise its historic origins (see pages 61–3).

Above left: 102. Groves & Whitnall's beers were at the heart of the arsenic controversy (see pages 63–6).

Above middle: 103. Hull was a fishing port with a dark drinking past (see pages 68–70).

Above right: 104. Hull Mild was so popular it was bottled as mild rather than brown ale.

One of the Hull Brewery Company's fleet of vehicles recently supplied by Cornelius Parish Ltd., Austin Distributors, Hull. The tank is of 20 barrels capacity and is mounted on an Austin 5 Ton 160″ Long Wheelbase petrol engined Chassis Cab.

105. Six more 20-barrel Austin tankers were added to the Hull Brewery fleet in 1960, but the accelerating switch to filtered bulk beer was later to cause conflict with CAMRA (see page 69).

JENNINGS BREWERY, COCKERMOUTH

106. Mount Charlotte also tried to take over Jennings Brewery of Cockermouth, but was beaten off (see page 73).

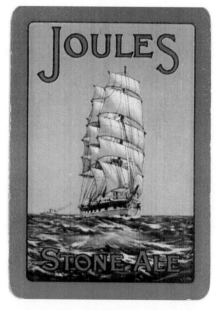

Above left: 107. Joule's boosted its profile with many eye-catching posters (Photo: Mike Peterson).

Above right: 108. Joule's beer was shipped from Liverpool to the United States (see pages 74–6).

Top right: 109. Long's had a shining reputation for its Gold Cup Ale (see page 77).

Below left: 110. A Little Bricky character was introduced in the 1960s to lift sales (see pages 76–8).

Bottom left: 111. Magee's liked to boast that they were also brewers in Burton-on-Trent (see pages 78–9).

Bottom right: 112. Hull Brewery also linked its Double Stout with oysters (see page 80).

Above left: 113. Rats were a constant problem in old breweries, as this 1904 poster from Noakes of London implies. Some may have slipped into the beer (see pages 82–4).

Above right: 114. Meux's powerful Imperial London Stout was supplied to Windsor Castle (see pages 84–6).

Left: 115. Posters proudly proclaimed that 'The liquid legend returns' (see pages 86–9).

Above left: 116. Under Whitbread, Castle Eden Ale became a national real ale.

Above right: 117. Nimmo's XXXX rose from the dead to celebrate the brewery's survival.

118. Oakhill Stout was promoted as a healthy option (see pages 89–90). Later the revived Old Brewery, Oakhill, produced a Velvet Stout (above).

119. Dutton's strong ale was known as Old Ben on draught, but bottled as OBJ (see pages 91–4).

120. To a small child, Whitaker's crowing cockerel could look quite scary at night (see page 94).

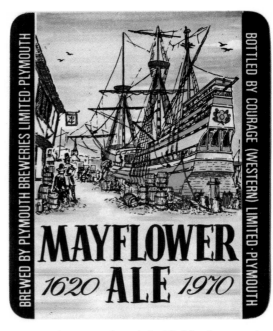

Above left: 121. Old Ram was only sold within 30 miles of the Halifax brewery (see pages 94–6).

Above right: 122. Mayflower Ale marked the merger of Plymouth and Courage (see pages 96–7).

123. The end of the dark ages in Devon – new Plymouth breweries like Plympton, set up in 1984, preferred to produce lighter bitters (see pages 96–7).

Above left: 124. Ratliffe's Stout label.

Above right: 125. Crabbers' Nip could surprise visitors to Cornwall (see pages 100–2).

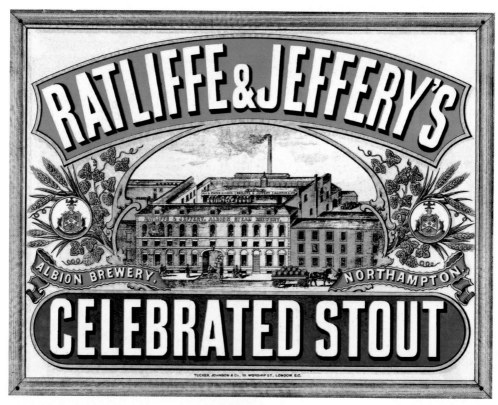

126. Ratliffe & Jeffery's were known for their Celebrated Stout (Picture: Alaric Neville) (see page 98).

127 & 128. Redruth powered to national prominence with its Newquay Steam beers (see pages 100–2).

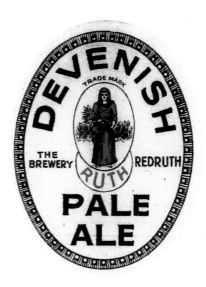

Above left: 129. Cornish Rebellion could not prevent Redruth's final closure in 2004 (see page 102).

Above right: 130. 'Red Ruth' survived on the Redruth labels until the 1960s (see page 101).

Above left: 131. Baltic breweries like Faxe of Denmark produced their own Imperial Stouts (see page 105).

Above right: 132. Courage's Imperial Russian Stout bowed out in 1993 – only to reappear in 2011 (see pages 104–6).

Above left: 133. After the takeover, Greenall Whitley blanded down Shipstone's Bitter (see pages 106–8).

Above right: 134. Simonds' pale ales followed the troops around the world (see pages 109–11).

H. & G. SIMONDS. L^{TD}..

Brewers.

READING.

THE HOP LEAF

135. Simonds' waterside site in Reading ensured good early transport links by barge (see pages 109–11).

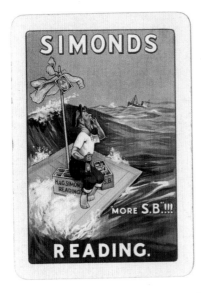

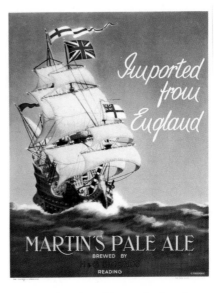

Above left: 136. In 1926 a comic film was made of a shipwrecked sailor to promote SB (see page 110).

Above right: 137. Simonds brewed a strong pale for Belgian importers John Martin of Antwerp (see page 110).

Above left: 138. Strong's promoted the Strong Country with signs along the railway lines.

Above right: 139. The company also produced guidebooks to the Strong Country (see pages 111–13).

Above left: 140. Whitbread revived the Strong Country name for a new cask bitter in 1980 (see page 112).

Above right: 141. Besides Watney's, other brewers outside Yorkshire with a Stingo in their tale included Adey & White of St Albans (see pages 113–15).

Above left: 142. Danny Blyth was converted to Crown Special at the end of the road to Pontyclun (see pages 116–18).

Above right: 143. The Clubs Brewery also supplied bottled beer from 1930 (Picture: John Hopkins).

Above left: 144. Hancock's called on John Bull to promote its beer in 1926 (Picture: John Hopkins) (see pages 118–20).

Above right: 145. The brewery dropped its long clubs title and changed to just Crown Brewery in 1976 (see page 117).

146. Hancock's used its dray horses to present an olde worlde image (see pages 118–20).

Above left: 147. Coal trains regularly rumbled past Rhymney Brewery, as shown on this service medal.

Above right: 148. The bottled beers were all produced at Crosswell's in Cardiff (see pages 121–22).

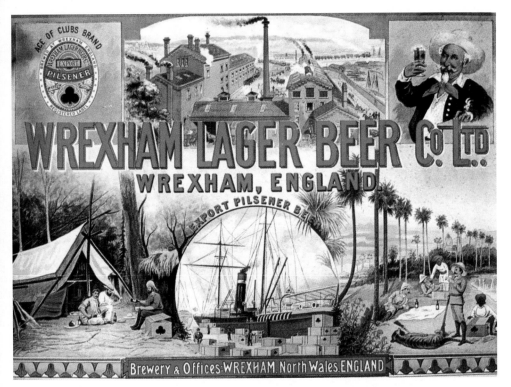

149. Wrexham Lager followed the flag round the globe to find a market (see pages 141–3).

150. Barclay's of London brewed light and dark lagers from 1921, after failing to takeover Wrexham (see page 142).

Above left: 151. Wrexham tried to build trade at home by issuing leaflets showing how to serve lager (see pages 141–3).

Above right: 152. Aitken's also enjoyed substantial trade in Glasgow, with its own office and stores (see pages 144–6).

153. Thomas Aitken's Victoria Bitter became the best-selling beer in Australia (see pages 145–6).

Above left: 154. Aitken's proudly featured the many medals won by its beers in its 1940 brochure (see pages 144–6).

Above right: 155. Caledonian's Deuchar's IPA was 'a bit cheeky' in using the Deuchar's name (see pages 146–8).

156. Robert Deuchar was able to pick up the Duddingston Brewery cheaply.

157. Other leading Edinburgh brewers like McEwan's were embarrassed by the court case (see pages 148–50).

Above left: 158. Jeffrey's continued to dish up Disher's Extra Strong Ale, but the brew had lost its sparkle (Label: Andrew Cunningham) (see page 150).

Above right: 159. Oat Malt Stout became 'The Pride of the Thistle Brewery' again in the 1990s (see pages 151–3).

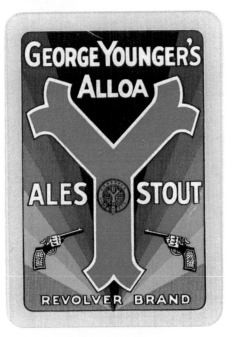

Above left: 160. George Younger fired his business through exports under the Revolver Brand (see pages 153–5).

Above right: 161. In the 1950s George Younger tried to build up trade at home.

Above left: 162. Still smiling – Hollywood starlet Venetia Stevenson on Sweetheart Stout (see page 155).

Above right: 163. Father William enjoys a bottle of No. 3 (see pages 155–8).

164. William Younger built up a substantial pub trade in the heart of London (see page 155).

165. Old soldiers never die – and neither did Younger's No. 3 as it was revived again in 2012 (see pages 155–8).

For a start it was well away from the London head office and largely left to manage its own affairs. It was also highly traditional, using wooden barrels long after most had switched to metal, open fermenting rounds and dry-hopping its best bitter. It even still delivered to local pubs by horse-drawn drays. Chairman Mr R. W. R. Law had proudly told the 1966 AGM, 'Our draught beer, matured in wood according to tradition, is highly praised and is brewed from the highest quality of malt and hops available.' The firm had only launched a keg beer, PB Superkeg, in 1969, including a dark Superkeg Mild.

The Regent Brewery was also, by national standards, quite tiny, producing just 1300 barrels a week, allowing it to handle limited production runs. As Courage admitted:

> The relatively small size of the Regent Brewery enables the organisation to retain the family atmosphere which existed here nearly 100 years ago. The whole staff, from the head brewer down, know each other personally ... the value of this relationship becomes particularly apparent in the peak summer months when brewing continues non-stop for 12 weeks at a stretch.

The same leaflet highlighted 'the famous Heavy, the dark beer brewed especially for, and unique to, the West Country'. Heavy was beginning to experience a bounce. Though it had a weak original gravity of 1032 (around 3% alcohol), it was full of flavour. Unlike most dark milds which add caramel to give a sweet taste, it owed its colour to using roasted barley to deliver a nutty, dry flavour. Carl Beeson of local craft brewer Summerskills called it 'a cross between a mild and a porter'.

Drinkers miles from Devon were starting to take notice. At CAMRA's Great British Beer Festival in London in 1979, Heavy received a special award. Many believe it would have been named Champion Mild or even Beer of the Year, but the beer sold so well there was not a drop left for the final judging panel!

However, hopes of a revival were torpedoed by Courage's decision to close the brewery and drop Heavy. Licensee Jack Sorrell of the Royal Marine, Efford, told the *Western Evening Herald* on 13 March 1984 after the last brew, 'I'm sorry to see the Heavy mild go because it has been one of the institutions over the 40 or 50 years I have been in the trade.'

Only the heavy horses lived on, as Courage decided to retain a pair of Shires in the port to soothe the loss of the brewery and its beers.

ODD BUT TRUE: The merger of Plymouth Breweries and Courage in 1970 was signalled by a special bottled beer, Mayflower Ale, marking the 350th anniversary of the sailing of the Pilgrim Fathers from Plymouth. It was brewed at the Regent Brewery but bottled by Courage.

BEER: Ratliffe's Stout
BREWER: Phipps of Northampton
ALSO KNOWN FOR: IPA and Number 10
BREWERY LOGO: Northampton's coat of arms, showing two lions on either side of a castle tower. Also a diamond and later a star.
HISTORIC RIVAL: Jumbo Stout from NBC
SIMILAR BREWS TODAY: Ratliffe's Celebrated Stout
ILLUSTRATIONS: 124, 126, 178-81

RATLIFFE'S STOUT: Breweries liked powerful beasts as their emblems. Horses, stags and bulls were popular, as were more exotic lions, tigers and elephants. Even unicorns. Nicholson's of Maidenhead rode its luck with a galloping camel. Eagles and hawks flew high in esteem. Some thought smaller as long as the creatures were endearing, like badgers, hares or squirrels. But only one dared adopt the rat.

The name of one of the brewery's founders explains why. But the company only cuddled up to the hated rodent when it became surprisingly popular during the Second World War.

Thomas Ratliffe and William Jeffery launched the Albion Brewery in Northampton in 1862. It proved successful, as was demonstrated by its grand Crown and Anchor Maltings, built on the banks of the River Nene in the 1880s. When it became a limited company in 1895 it owned 135 pubs and was valued at £250,000. But the untimely death of William Jeffery the same year led to the larger Northampton brewery of Phipps, founded in Towcester in 1801, taking control in 1899. The Albion Brewery soon closed, with production concentrated at Phipps' Bridge Street premises.

Thomas Ratliffe and his son Richard both became Phipps' directors and ensured their family name was not forgotten by local drinkers thanks to a stout memorial. Signs on the town's pubs now proclaimed 'Phipps' Noted Ales and Ratliffe's Celebrated Stout'. The 'Rat' was not to be easily exterminated.

Phipps were the dominant local brewers, having built a new brewery in the 1860s using the Burton Union system of fermentation. Two family members were elected mayors of Northampton and one also became a local MP. When the business was made a limited company in 1880, it was valued at £500,000. According to Mike Brown's Brewery History Society directory of the county's brewers, *Brewed in Northants*, 'By 1892 the Bridge Street Brewery had the largest tied estate of any Midlands brewery and the ninth largest in Britain.' Trade extended into Coventry and Birmingham.

This was the considerable company the Ratliffes had joined in 1899, with Thomas Ratliffe becoming joint managing director. But the Rats had joined a stinking ship. There were serious splits in the boardroom over strategy. Even worse, the quality of the beer had dramatically deteriorated after the head brewer left to start up his own brewery. A consultant brought in to examine the problem came to the damning conclusion, 'I'm sorry to say it, but you haven't a barrel of beer in your cellars fit to send out.'

The company's 'Celebrated Diamond Ales' were far from sparkling and to add to their woes, Burton giants Bass were objecting to their use of the diamond design. It couldn't get worse, but it did. The firm's Towcester brewery burnt down in 1901. Trade was pouring away and the share price slumped.

After a crisis EGM in 1903 forced the resignation of one of the managing directors, the drilling of a new well to improve water quality and the modernisation of the brewing plant, the situation slowly improved. But tensions were still high. In 1906 the new MD, Louis Walker, was sacked for 'insolent behaviour' towards the autocratic chairman Pickering Phipps. Walker later became the boss of major Burton brewers Ind Coope.

Thomas Ratliffe died in 1927, but after Pickering Phipps' death ten years later, his son Richard Ratliffe became chairman and managing director. He was to preside over 'Little Rat's' finest hour. That was the popular name for a bottle of Ratliffe's Stout. It gnawed its way into the nation's consciousness during the Second World War when it was shipped out to the Northamptonshire Regiment serving in North Africa to help keep up morale among the famous 'Desert Rats'. Never mind *Ice Cold in Alex*, a Little Rat at El Alamein was just as welcome.

After the war the armoured division's red rat emblem was added to the label for Ratliffe's Stout. In case drinkers did not swallow the connection, the rat posed in front of a desert palm tree and a pyramid. But it was to be a brief moment in the sun. Little Rat was about to be crushed by a lumbering Jumbo.

Phipps had taken over Manning's Castle Brewery in Northampton in 1933, followed by Campbell Praed of Wellingborough in 1954, bringing the total number of houses to more than 700. But three years later came the really big deal, when Phipps merged with the neighbouring Northampton Brewery Company. Only an 18-inch brick wall had separated the breweries. The merger added an extra 420 pubs to create one of the largest tied estates of the time in England of over 1,100. It now totally dominated the area.

But the move proved a Rat trap. The combined company adopted NBC's star sign as its logo and in the rationalisation of the beer range that followed, Little Rat was trampled to death by NBC's sweeter Jumbo Stout, which was initially rebranded as Ratliffe's Jumbo Stout, with an original gravity of 1035. A new Bison Brown Ale thundered in and a top-fermented Stein Lager was launched in 1959.

A further 150 pubs were bought from Ind Coope, but its large estate made Phipps NBC a takeover target. In 1960 it joined London brewer Watney's growing Red Barrel empire. By 1968 Phipps had become Watney Mann (Midlands) with the Northampton breweries closing within a few years. The buildings were replaced by a huge Carlsberg brewery. Jumbo was forgotten – but not Little Rat.

Helped by former Phipps brewers like Pat Heron, brothers Alaric and Quentin Neville revived the famous name. After first bringing back Phipps IPA from the dead, they had Ratliffe's Celebrated Stout brewed by Tony Davis at the Grainstore Brewery in Rutland in 2009, based on the pre-war recipes. With a strength of 4.3%, it is described as 'dark and mellow' with 'distinctive roasted flavours'. Drinkers are urged to 'open a bottle and turn back the hands of time'. And on the back label are two red rats in the desert.

ODD BUT TRUE: The Northampton Brewery Company's distant properties included the Molineux estate in Wolverhampton. In 1890 the firm leased part of the grounds to Wolverhampton Wanderers FC to play football, before selling the site to them in 1901.

BEER: Redruth Pale
BREWER: Redruth Brewery, Cornwall
ALSO KNOWN FOR: Home Brew, Bardic Ale and Crabbers' Nip
BREWERY LOGO: Woman carrying barley and later an heraldic tiger holding a cross
HISTORIC RIVAL: Duchy Pale Ale from St Austell Brewery
SIMILAR BREWS TODAY: Tribute from St Austell Brewery
ILLUSTRATIONS: 125, 127-30, 182, 183

REDRUTH PALE: It wasn't the usual new beer launch. We were flown to Newquay in a small plane to see a range of 'steam beers' in old-fashioned swing-stoppered bottles. Head brewer Tony Wharmby – the 'Head of Steam' – guided us through seven different brews, from light bitters to extra-strong lagers. They were said to be 'the first complete range of entirely natural beers to be brewed anywhere in the world', extending the German beer purity laws over English brown ales and an Irish-style stout.

But this 'New Age of Steam' in 1987 was just one surprise in Redruth's roller-coaster ride, which saw the company regularly change identity. Only the year before the Devenish Redruth Brewery had become the Cornish Brewery. And there were bigger upheavals to come in the future – when Redruth was to be controlled from China.

Its roots were dug deep into the area's extensive tin mining industry. The Wickett family who came to control the brewery were also involved in mining. Redruth derives its Cornish name (rhyd – ford, ruth – red) from how the metal workings discoloured local streams. But the brewery had its own water supply, a bore hole called the Buller. It was known for its bottled pale ales, as well as its rich brown ale, Home Brew.

In the early 1930s the Wickett family ran into trouble with shareholders. One returned from Australia to pursue his case and the family was advised to sell up or risk jail. In 1934 Devenish of Weymouth in Dorset took a controlling interest. The miners' brewery had joined distinguished company.

Devenish had been awarded an unprecedented five Royal Warrants. The coats of arms of princes, dukes and kings decorated the seaside company's beer labels and price lists. It was claimed that this royal connection began in 1872 when the Prince of Wales (later King Edward VII) called at Weymouth on the Royal Yacht and was so impressed by Devenish's Pale Ale that he appointed them brewers to his household.

Devenish had already sailed into Cornwall, having taken over Carne's Brewery in Falmouth in 1921, followed by Mallett's of Truro two years later. But the Redruth takeover gave it a much bigger presence, later consolidated by adding houses from the Treluswell Brewery near Penryn in 1943. Production for the county was concentrated at Redruth, supplying around 200 pubs.

Until the 1960s Redruth maintained its distinct identity, with a cloaked 'Red Ruth' lady on the labels. A member of the Wickett family was still managing director in the late 1950s. But after Devenish merged with its Weymouth neighbour Groves in 1960, the group was reorganised under the Devenish name. An emblem of an heraldic tiger holding a cross (popularly known as Herbert) was introduced in 1965, adapted from the Devenish family crest, and all the pubs were repainted in green, gold and white.

The product range was rationalised. Redruth Pale Ale became Green Top and then in 1972 Wessex Pale Ale in bottle and Wessex or Cornish Best Bitter on draught. With an original gravity of 1042.5, Cornish was described as 'smooth and full-bodied'. Saxon replaced High Life as the group's keg beer in 1969. A top-fermented Viking 'Lager' was added in 1973. Many speciality beers were dropped, though the delightfully named Crabbers' Nip strong ale remained in the pool to catch the unwary until 1982.

The business was hampered by its highly seasonal trade. Particularly Redruth. In the tourist county of Cornwall, 60% of its annual trade was done in just fourteen weeks over summer. At Redruth this meant they brewed just once a week in February, but every day of the week in August. Its best-selling brew was just as unusual.

Devenish followed a West Country tradition. Its bread-and-butter beer was a low-gravity well-hopped 'boys' bitter with an original gravity of just 1032, known as 'ordinary', though it was given the grander title of John Devenish Bitter in 1983. Although almost as weak as a harvest ale, it was the company's big profit-maker. This restricted moves to bring in a more standard-strength bitter.

The Devenish brewery in Weymouth had already suffered during the Second World War, when it was bombed out of action for almost two years. In 1985 it was closed for good when all production was concentrated at Redruth. But there was a bigger bombshell waiting in the wings. The company was still largely family run by the Ludlow brothers Bill and Michael. But after a merger with ambitious pub group Inn Leisure in 1986, the chain's chief Michael Cannon took control, forcing out the Ludlows. He was to shake up the beer business.

Wessex was relaunched as Wessex Stud. A new Cornish Original (1038) and the provocatively named GBH (Great British Heavy) strong ale (1050) were introduced. The imaginative range of Newquay Steam bottled beers was followed by canned and keg versions, a Steam Bitter on draught and a Prohibition low-alcohol lager. An export division was set up to sell half the production abroad within a few years.

But Cannon fired up a storm with plans to close some country pubs and to sell town centre houses for shops. And hopes of exporting Steam to America were thwarted after the Anchor Steam Brewery of San Francisco objected. A Churchill range had to be introduced instead. Within a few years the renamed Cornish Brewery was running out of steam. Speculation mounted that the unprofitable site would be shut, despite a modern plant having been installed from the closed Wilson's Brewery in Manchester.

In 1991 the Boddingtons Pub Company launched a £127 million takeover bid. It failed, but prompted parent company Devenish to allow a surprise management buyout of the brewery led by managing director Paul Smith, while Whitbread took over the beer brands including Newquay Steam.

The Redruth Brewery name returned, but there was no cask beer, apart from Cornish Original for Whitbread, as Redruth now had no pubs. But a keg and canned John Davey's Cornish Bitter was produced, named after the founder of the brewery in 1742. The bulk of the business was brewing and packaging for supermarkets and others and the profit margins proved too tight. The venture went into receivership in 1994. It looked as doomed as in 1991, but again rose from the dead.

The Dransfield Group of Hong Kong, which also ran the Yixing Brewery near Shanghai, bought Redruth in 1995 for £2 million. The intention was to use it as a training centre for its Chinese staff, as well as producing Yixing lager in the UK and specialist bottled beers like the American-style Indianhead and Screamin' Beaver.

But Redruth also tried to rebuild its links at home. Its logo featured a lamb and the Cornish flag. In 1998 it reintroduced cask beers including Crofty Bitter (3.6%), named after the last tin mine in Cornwall, and the flagship Cornish Rebellion (4.8%). There was even a Steam Brewed Bitter (5%). Cornish Original (4.1%) also bounced back on the bar, based on the original pale ale recipe, as well as a Miners' Mild (3.6%).

But the Crofty mine had just closed and Redruth was unable to avoid the same fate for a third time in 2004, when the company went into administration. Its lack of pubs had told in the end. Michael Cannon had sold off the Devenish estate to another pub company in 1993 for £214 million.

ODD BUT TRUE: Devenish gained the Wessex brand when it bought Vallance's of Sidmouth in Devon in 1957 from Woodhead's, who ran the South London Brewery in Southwark. The London firm was an unusual act. Controlled by Irish brewer Beamish of Cork and theatrical impresario Prince Littler, it did stout trade in theatre bars.

BEER: Royal Commemoration Ale
BREWER: Royal Brewery, Brentford, London
ALSO KNOWN FOR: Royal Stout and Light Bitter Ale
BREWERY LOGO: The royal coat of arms
HISTORIC RIVAL: William Gomm's Beehive Brewery, Brentford
ILLUSTRATIONS: 184, 185

ROYAL COMMEMORATION ALE: This is a beer you're extremely unlikely to have ever tasted. Nor is it one of the many bottled beers produced to mark various royal weddings, silver jubilees or coronations. Just to add to the confusion, it was brewed thirty-four years after the brewery closed. Yet the Brewery Tap still serves pints today and the name of the brewer involved is still firmly on the map – in Canada. It also lives on in spirit on bottles of London's other famous alcoholic tipple.

The prime figure in this royal intrigue was Felix Booth, who in the 1820s ran the Red Lion Brewery in Brentford and a distillery on the opposite side of the High Street, famous for Booth's London Gin, founded by his family around 1740. It was a time when the Government was moving to curb the wild excesses of the capital's notorious 'gin palaces' by favouring 'more wholesome' beer. With his feet firmly planted in both drinks markets, Felix Booth was well placed to ride out the storm. He was a wealthy and eminent man, being made the Sheriff of London in 1828.

That year he donated the princely sum of £17,000 towards John Ross's Arctic expedition in search of the legendary Northwest Passage around the American continent, following a meeting with the then Prince William in Brentford, after the Government had refused to support the venture.

It proved to be money well spent. When he succeeded to the throne, King William IV visited the brewery in 1832 and rewarded the generosity of Felix Booth with a royal warrant. The Red Lion Brewery's name was changed to the Royal Brewery and the royal coat of arms hung above the entrance. Captain Ross also honoured Sir Felix (he was made a Baronet in 1835) by scattering his patron's name across the frozen continent. The most northerly peninsula of the American mainland, north of Hudson Bay, is still called Boothia today. There's also a Cape Felix and a Brentford Bay.

But the royal warrant was unusual. It was permanent and did not expire on the death of the monarch who had granted it, a distinction which the brewery claimed it only shared with The Dome in Brighton. Its legitimacy was challenged in 1904, but it was upheld and the company continued to vigorously defend its right to the honour – even after the brewery closed in 1923, following its takeover by Style & Winch of Kent.

So keen were directors within Courage and Barclay (who had absorbed Style & Winch in 1929) to maintain this flattering royal connection, that in 1957 they produced a Royal Brewery Commemoration Ale in a corked bottle to mark the 125th anniversary of the warrant. The label featured the royal coat of arms and scenes from Ross's Arctic expedition, which had discovered the position of the magnetic North Pole in 1831.

The expanding brewing group clung on to its royal connection for years, the Royal Brewery Company only being formally liquidated in 1970. Bottles of Commemoration Ale lingered even longer, still being eagerly sought by collectors today – but they wouldn't dare open one and taste a drop. The bottles are far too valuable.

It was a potent brew, probably based on Style & Winch's powerful barley wine from Maidstone. And certainly far removed from the lighter beers the Royal Brewery promoted before the First World War. It had become a limited company in 1890 with 102 pubs under the chairmanship of Kent hop grower Montague Ballard – and proved just as pioneering as any Arctic explorer.

A Royal Brewery booklet boasted, 'The company can certainly claim for a recently introduced speciality that they are far ahead of most breweries in the production of their Light Bitter Ale, having placed on the market a unique novelty in the form of an absolutely non-deposit beer.' These bright, filtered bottled beers only began to replace sediment beers after 1900.

'The process of manufacture may be described as an entirely new departure in the brewing industry, being practically an amalgamation of the American and German lager beer principles,' added the booklet. 'This beer is specially brewed for supplying the family trade. It is contemplated, owing to the ever-increasing demand, to erect and fit up a still larger brewery, in order to cope with this growing trade.'

The Royal Brewery was also an early believer in improved public houses offering food, promoting its dignified premises before the First World War under the slogans 'Sensible Houses for Sensible Men' and 'Pleasant Public Houses for the People'.

The Graphic, in a 1909 profile of The Forester in West Ealing, commented:

> The Forester, which was only opened the other day, is solidly built and is of most artistic design. Its restaurant, saloon, private and public bars are all cheery and pleasant places, panelled in mahogany and oak and handsomely furnished, with capacious cellars beneath built of the best white-glazed bricks.
>
> Great care has been bestowed upon the heating, ventilating and lighting and the comfort of visitors has been carefully studied. Here the working man can take his dinner or enjoy his glass of beer in cheerful surroundings. Daily and illustrated papers are supplied.

Pictures showed potted ferns and vases of flowers in the elegant Working Man's Bar. These 'Sensible Houses for Sensible Men' did not encourage insensible drinking, though some, like The Nelson in Twickenham, were later known as 'Royal Stout Houses' after another of the company's brews.

ODD BUT TRUE: After Felix Booth's death in 1850, the Royal Brewery was acquired by a Mr Carrington, whose son Richard also became a famous explorer – of outer space. He established an observatory at Redhill in 1854 to study the stars and sun spots.

BEER: Russian Imperial Stout
BREWER: Barclay Perkins, Anchor Brewery, Southwark, London
ALSO KNOWN FOR: Barclay's Lager, Doctor Brown Ale and No. 1 Southwarke Ale
BREWERY LOGO: Dr Johnson
HISTORIC RIVAL: Reid's XX Imperial, Camden, London
SIMILAR BREWS TODAY: Harvey's Imperial Extra Double Stout, Lewes, Sussex, and Pitfield's 1792 Imperial Stout, Epping, Essex
ILLUSTRATIONS: 1, 131, 132, 186-8

RUSSIAN IMPERIAL STOUT: If you peer into the depths of a dark glass of beer, your imagination can conjure up the strangest images and the tallest tales. Perhaps that's why one of London's greatest breweries, Barclay Perkins, has such strong literary connections. The pen was always firmly dipped in its pint pot.

The scholar Samuel Johnson once even lived at the Anchor Brewery and advised the Thrale family on the sale of the business in 1781 to Robert Barclay of the banking dynasty and brewery manager John Perkins, famously saying, 'We are not here to sell a parcel of boilers and vats, but the potentiality of growing rich beyond the dreams of avarice.' He was right. It sold for £135,000, a fortune in those days. But the price matched the potential, as by 1815 Barclay Perkins was the leading brewer in London, producing more than 330,000 barrels a year. And its flagship beer was 'Russian'.

Russian Imperial Stout was originally produced by the London brewers as an 'extra stout' porter for export to the Baltic countries from the late eighteenth century. The powerful brew gained its name from supplying the Russian imperial court. The artist Joseph Farington wrote in his diary in 1796, 'I drank some porter Mr Lindoe had from Thrale's brewhouse [The brewery was still known as Thrale's years after Barclay's takeover]. He said it was specially brewed for the Empress of Russia [Catherine the Great].'

Barclays' Russian Imperial Stout became the classic example of the style. A recipe from 1856 shows it had an original gravity of 1107 (well over 10% alcohol) with a resounding smack of more than 10lbs of hops to the barrel, which ensured it kept well during the sea voyages. It was shipped to the Baltic ports in huge hogsheads (54-gallon casks). Enterprising middlemen like Belgium-born London beer merchant, Albert Le Coq, also bottled it for sale overseas. In 1974 Norwegian divers recovered bottles from the 1869 shipwreck of the Olivia in the Baltic. They were stamped 'A Le Coq'. Sadly, seawater damage prevented a tasting of the 105-year-old vintage beer.

Victorian authors could not resist pouring Barclay's celebrated porter into their books. Charles Dickens was intoxicated by its beers, with many references. Dick Swiveller claimed in the *Old Curiosity Shop*, published in 1840, that there was 'a spell in every drop against the ills of mortality'. It was a job at Barclay's Brewery that Micawber had in mind when he was 'waiting for something to turn up'.

Barclay's Imperial was so successful that Russian and Eastern European brewers imitated the brew. Even Danish lager giant Carlsberg began brewing a Gammel (old) Porter Imperial Stout. Albert Le Coq was forced to buy a brewery in Tartu, Estonia, in 1910, in order to compete as the export market ebbed away before the First World War.

As they lost their overseas markets, most British brewers abandoned the style. But Barclay's kept the imperial flag flying by switching to supplying the home trade with a warming winter brew matured in bottle for at least a year at the brewery. Gift packs of the nip-size (third of a pint) bottles were introduced and occasionally it was sold in corked and wired 'champagne' quart bottles. Dr Johnson became the brewery's heavyweight trademark, with his face plastered over the bottle labels.

As a 1934 advert declared, 'Between this Russian Stout and ordinary stout there is as much difference as between a fine vintage port and a bottle of "three-

&-sixpenny".' Wine writer Cyril Ray described it as 'a smooth, rich, velvety depth-charge of a drink'. And the maturation period grew longer. In 1953, when vintage labels were introduced, the first was for the 1949 batch.

After Barclay Perkins merged with Courage in 1955, production moved to Courage's brewery by Tower Bridge, with the Courage name taking over on the label. The Anchor Brewery closed in 1964 when the Globe bottling plant was built on the site.

The Globe name reflected the deep heritage of the area. It wasn't just Dr Johnson who had written himself into the brewery's history. Shakespeare's Globe Theatre originally stood on the Anchor premises before burning down in 1613. In 1909 a bronze plaque had been unveiled on the brewery wall in Park Street, commemorating the fact. And when Barclay's produced a Festival Ale in 1951 to mark the nearby Festival of Britain, the Globe Theatre was featured on the label.

When Courage's plant also closed, brewing moved out of London in 1982 to John Smith's of Tadcaster in Yorkshire. The imperial legend was gradually being lost inside a giant brewing combine. Brews became every few years, with the last in 1993, ending more than 200 years of rich liquid history, as Courage itself was swallowed by a succession of international groups.

However, in 2007 Wells and Young's of Bedford bought the neglected Courage brands and in 2011 relaunched Russian Imperial Stout. It was a labour of love for head brewer Jim Robertson, who had worked for Courage when it was brewed in London. The black treacly brew (10%) was back to warm drinkers again. Though, as befitting its history, it was initially only sold abroad, mainly in the USA.

ODD BUT TRUE: Barclay's Brewery was one of the sights of London in the nineteenth century. Even kings and emperors flocked to see the towering vessels. But one visit sparked an international incident. The Austrian General Haynau was notorious for the brutality with which he put down rebellions in Hungary and Italy. When word spread that the 'Hyena' had arrived in 1850, brewery workers attacked him with sticks and stones. Haynau was forced to flee. The Austrian ambassador demanded an apology, but the Foreign Secretary Lord Palmerston said the men were just 'expressing their feelings at what they considered inhuman conduct'. When the Italian revolutionary Garibaldi visited Britain in 1864, he insisted on visiting the brewery to thank the workers.

BEER: Shipstone's Bitter
BREWER: James Shipstone and Sons founded in New Basford, Nottingham, in 1852.
ALSO KNOWN FOR: Shipstone's Mild
BREWERY LOGO: A six-point star
HISTORIC RIVAL: Home Bitter from the Home Brewery of Daybrook
SIMILAR BREWS TODAY: Star Bitter from the Belvoir Brewery of Old Dalby in Leicestershire, which was set up by former Shipstone's brewer Colin Brown in 1995.
ILLUSTRATIONS: 133, 189, 190

SHIPSTONE'S BITTER: When the chairman of Northern Foods, Nicholas Horsley, was desperately trying to take over Shipstone's Star Brewery in 1978, he admitted, 'Shipstone's beer is very good and we would probably sell it in our pubs.' The food group already owned the Hull Brewery.

His plea was in vain. It was never going to sway shareholders who knew his £13.5 million offer was a cheap shot. He only picked up a derisory 1.9% of shares. The *Nottingham Evening Post* celebrated Horsley's defeat: 'There are times when a pint of Shippo's [as the beers were affectionately known] tastes better than a glass of Pol Roger [vintage champagne]'.

Many Nottingham people agreed; 20,000 had signed CAMRA's 'Save Our Shippo's' petition. The distinctive bitter and dark mild were revered. The campaign's *Nottingham and Derby Drinker* magazine said after the victory that 'to many people, Shippo's beer is the Nottingham taste of beer – something too important to lose'.

They were much more bitter than most Midlands brews. And the sharp smack of the hops echoed far beyond the region and Shipstone's 250 pubs. *Guardian* columnist Richard Boston commented in his 1976 book *Beer and Skittles*, 'It is easy to catch the enthusiasm expressed by locals for the mild and bitter, both very well-flavoured.'

Their reputation had been built on the sandstone beneath the brewery in Basford, which provided quality brewing water as well as cool caves for storage. Their profile was enhanced by the towering brewhouse built on the six-acre Radford Road site in 1900, its star-shaped clock becoming a local landmark. The grand offices next door were known for their mahogany panelling and sweeping staircase.

The family were sticklers for tradition. They stuck to wooden casks made in their own cooperage long after most brewers had switched to metal containers. Chairman James Shipstone proudly told the AGM in 1967, 'All our draught beers are served only from the wood, as has always been our practice ... the public seem to like it that way.'

Shippo's also nuzzled its way into local hearts by continuing to use dray horses for deliveries. And not just any horses, but striking greys, a special cross-breed, half Shire and half Percheron or Suffolk Punch. Before 1914 they had almost 240 in their extensive stables – then most went off to war and, like many soldiers, never returned. But the noble ranks were built back up to over eighty by 1926. There were still twenty-seven in harness in 1962, stopping the city traffic and entrancing the public.

Head brewer Jim Mackness, who joined the company in 1949, was proud of his beer. 'We use only top-quality malt. We don't touch any adjuncts, not even flaked maize. We only add a little crystal malt to the bitter and mild and use a small amount of sugar.'

But he admitted Shipstone's Bitter (4% alcohol) had a reputation for 'Shippo's head' the morning after – which he put down to the yeast. 'It is a very strong strain. It dates back to 1900.' One drinker called it 'the unpredictable Basford strangler'. As the *Evening Post* said at the time of the Northern Foods bid, 'It's a distinctive beer. You can't be indifferent to it.' You either loved it or loathed it. But admirers were devoted.

But there were also other admirers within the industry. Just a few weeks after Horsley's defeat, Britain's biggest regional brewer, Greenall Whitley of Warrington, made a £20 million bid in May 1978 and the deal was swiftly sealed. Shippo's had sold its soul.

The chill winds of change had been blowing through the business, as the family lost control. The costly wooden casks had been rolled out of use after 1970. Horse deliveries ended in the same year. Shipstone's was finding trade a struggle. It was losing many pubs to slum clearances.

Chairman Robert Combe said in 1978 that 'in the last 15 years we have lost 75 out of 300 due to redevelopment and only been able to build 25.' New pubs were expensive, costing around £250,000 each, and Shipstone's was short of cash. Many of their surviving pubs were in poor repair. Production was down to 160,000 barrels a year.

Greenall's arrival had a major impact. 'You can't go anywhere in Nottingham these days without being bombarded with the name of Shipstone,' said Peter Martin in a feature for CAMRA's national newspaper *What's Brewing* in September 1979.

'It seems as if most of the city's buses now have "Shipstone's local bitter" emblazoned on their upper decks, and when you turn on the radio the local commercial station is blasting out Shipstone's jingles.' Wayne Fontana of Mindbenders fame had been signed up to sing about 'my kind of pint'. It was a far cry from previous Shippo's marketing, involving a quaint cartoon figure called Ivor Thirst with a star-shaped head.

But drinkers' fears were being realised on two fronts. Nottingham had been noted for the cheapness of its beer. Prices had started to rise. More worryingly, the beer began to lose its bite. Greenall's admitted in 1981 that they had reduced the hop rate. Chris Holmes, who later developed the Castle Rock Brewery in the city, commented, 'Everyone who knew Shipstone's knew it as a fiendish brew with a strong local character. After the merger, it was blanded down to make it more acceptable.'

And the third unspoken fear came to pass in 1990, when Greenall's announced they were pulling out of brewing and closing Shipstone's Brewery with the loss of 200 jobs. GMB works convenor Graham Newbold said, 'Everybody is shell-shocked. There were a few of us in tears. We never expected this to happen.'

The last brew was early in 1991. Although a Shipstone's Bitter and Mild were produced by Allied Breweries for Greenall's until 1999, the shining star's reputation was dimmed long before the bitter end.

ODD BUT TRUE: After Greenall's shut the brewery in 1991, Nottingham Forest played in the FA Cup Final at Wembley with Shipstone's name across their shirts. The sponsorship gave the brewery its greatest publicity – just after its death.

BEER: Simonds Pale Ale
BREWER: H&G Simonds, Reading
ALSO KNOWN FOR: Berry Brown Ale and Old Berkshire Strong Ale
BREWERY LOGO: A red hop leaf
HISTORIC RIVAL: Alton Pale Ale from Hampshire
SIMILAR BREWS TODAY: Hop Leaf Pale Ale from Farsons of Malta
ILLUSTRATIONS: 134-7, 191-3

SIMONDS PALE ALE: No brewer tracked the armed forces so closely. In fact, its inside information was so good, some senior offices feared it might be a threat to national security. During summer manoeuvres in 1872 on Salisbury Plain, commanders followed sealed orders to reach a secret target – only to find Simonds' staff camped on the spot, barrels tapped, ready to slake the soldiers' thirst.

With such sound intelligence, Army chiefs soon decided it was best to formally enlist Simonds of Reading as their specialist suppliers. The move was to see Simonds follow the flag around the globe and win royal recognition. Though the company lost its independence in 1960, its Hop Leaf Pale Ale can still be found in some unexpected places – like Malta in the Mediterranean.

Simonds had military connections from its earliest years. When William Blackall Simonds inherited his father's farming, malting and brewing business in 1782, he also gained substantial land at Sandhurst – where the Royal Military College opened in 1813. The victory at Waterloo was soon toasted there in Simonds' beer.

The family also had strong political and financial interests. The eminent architect of the Bank of England, Sir John Soane, was commissioned in 1789 to design a new brewery in Bridge Street. A hop leaf on the office wallpaper was later adopted as the brewery trademark. In 1797 a Boulton & Watt steam engine was installed to power the plant.

It claimed to have spring water 'almost identical' to that of Burton and with its riverside location was by 1834 exporting pale ale as far as Australia. It began bottling in 1858. In addition to its strong, well-hopped IPA for distant lands, it also developed a lighter pale ale for the home market. Known as SB – Season's Brew – as it was originally brewed for summer, it was one of the first beers to have dry hops added in cask. SB became very popular, accounting for more than half of the 115,000 barrels produced annually by 1885. The Burton Union system of fermentation was introduced in the 1880s to ensure the quality of the beers.

This was no sleepy country concern, but an ambitious business – marching ahead with the British Army. It was well placed to supply the main Army base of Aldershot, established in 1855. It attacked the challenge with military precision, even setting up a department to make tents and field equipment for canvas canteens. The family were also closely involved in the Great Western Railway, and developed a wide rail ale trade supplying station buffets.

Wherever the Army went, Simonds followed under its slogan 'The Stuff for the Troops'. Branches were established in Gibraltar, Malta, Cyprus, Egypt and South Africa. The Malta trade began as early as 1875. The business advanced and retreated with the soldiers. Trade in Sudan, for example, launched in 1889, later had to be hurriedly withdrawn. Branches in Dublin and Cork supplying the British Army in Ireland were shut after being attacked during the rebellion. In the 1930s around half those employed at the brewery were ex-servicemen.

Simonds' expertise also allowed them to advance far beyond the military to other outside events like agricultural shows and sporting venues. They lubricated the British Empire Exhibition at Wembley in 1925 and a year later the Prince of Wales visited the brewery. He was particularly interested in the brewery wharf 'where beers in cask and large stacks of bottled beer were being loaded into barges for conveyance to London Docks for export', reported the first issue of Simonds' *Hop Leaf Gazette*.

Simonds were marketing innovators. In 1926 a comic film was made to promote SB in cinemas showing a shipwrecked sailor landing his raft on an island where he builds a wireless set out of a bottle case, using bottles as valves and a large shell as a speaker. A monkey erects the aerial in a palm tree. The thirsty sailor then broadcasts a plea for SB.

It was a call heard around the Empire, particularly since Simonds had been granted a Royal Warrant as brewers to King George V. And to ensure troops were supplied abroad, the firm invested in overseas breweries. In 1929 its Maltese agency merged with a new local brewery to form Simonds-Farsons. This meant Simonds' 'Hop Leaf' Pale Ale could be brewed on the island rather than being imported as a high-gravity beer before being diluted for sale. Later in 1948 this venture merged with a local lager brewery to create Simonds Farsons Cisk.

During the war Simonds-Farsons also ran a brewery in Tripoli for the NAAFI. Simonds ventured further into Africa in 1948, taking a substantial interest in East African Breweries of Kenya, Uganda and Tanganyika, famed for its Tusker lager. It linked up with Saccone & Speed of Gibraltar and also brewed a powerful pale ale with extra bite called Bulldog (6.3%) for export bottlers Robert Porter of London, as well as supplying another strong pale ale to Belgian importers John Martin of Antwerp.

At home its growing number of takeovers partly reflected this global vision, notably the Tamar Brewery in 1919 and the Octagon Brewery in 1954, both in the major naval port of Plymouth, as well as Rogers of Bristol in 1935. It was also one of the early pioneers of canned beer from a site in Southampton, initially to supply ships' stores. Later it took great pride in opening a pub, The Tavern in Reading, which only supplied canned beer 'served to the bars at cool cellar temperature on endless conveyors'.

Chairman Eric Simonds was also chairman of the Brewers' Society's Beer for Troops committee during the Second World War, with Simonds' London site in Wandsworth Road adopted as the central packing depot for dispatching more than 7.5 million bottles to the front line. A plaque was later erected on the building 'to commemorate one of the great features which sustained the morale and revived men whilst they defied the armed might of Germany'.

By the time it merged with Courage and Barclay of London in 1960, Simonds' domestic trade stretched across the South of England and into South Wales, with more than 1,200 pubs. Fittingly, its final chairman was a major military figure, General Sir Miles Dempsey, commander of the British Second Army in the 1944 landings in France.

Its best-known beer was its IPA, sold as Tavern Export in bottles and cans since 1950 and promoted by a happy hop leaf character called Hoppy. Tavern was swiftly adopted by the Courage group as the brand name for its national keg bitter.

The Simonds name soon slipped into history, with Reading becoming the headquarters of Courage Central. The town centre brewery was replaced in 1980 by a huge modern plant alongside the M4 at Worton Grange, focussing on producing Foster's lager. After a Simonds Bitter was briefly revived in the 1980s, the Hop Leaf was swept away. But it still pours abroad as a 'classic brew' on the island of Malta.

ODD BUT TRUE: In the 1957 Rank film *Doctor at Large* actor Donald Sinden is seen walking past a brewery with a large sign promoting 'Blarney's "Queen of the Bogs" Extra Strong Irish Ales'. The brewery was supposed to be in Cork, but was in fact Simonds' Surrey subsidiary, Ashby's of Staines.

BEER: Strong's Golden Ale
BREWER: Strong's, Romsey, Hampshire
ALSO KNOWN FOR: Rumsey Brown, Black Bess Stout and keg Barleycorn
BREWERY LOGO: A portcullis
HISTORIC RIVAL: Brickwood's Light Sunshine Ale from Portsmouth
SIMILAR BREWS TODAY: Red Shoot's New Forest Gold from Linwood or Boondoggle from Ringwood Brewery, both in Hampshire
ILLUSTRATIONS: 138-40, 194

STRONG'S GOLDEN ALE: Breweries like to be identified with their locality, but only one gave its name to a whole region. Visitors by road or rail to the area around the New Forest were greeted with signs stating 'Welcome to the Strong Country'. An arch over the brewery entrance proclaimed 'The Heart of the Strong Country'. But the beer which helped make the company's fortune was far from a strong ale, despite the old Hampshire saying 'so drunk, he must have been to Romsey.'

Strong's liked to claim that its Strong Country message was promoting tourism rather than its ale. 'All over this area you will see the famous pictorial poster "You're now in the Strong Country". Its subtlety is powerful in its effect. No mention, you notice, of Strong's beer. No plugging of any kind. Simply a statement of fact,' it boasted. 'No-one can tour in this area without having the fact indelibly impressed on his mind.'

But in the 1950s this subtle approach began to be soaked in Golden Ale, with the roadside signs now advising, 'In the Strong Country, they drink Strong's Golden Ale.' This light bitter ale was first brewed in the 1930s and swiftly satisfied public taste, said the brewery. It was promoted as a glass of liquid sunshine for the sunshine coast and, unusually, for women as well as men.

'Until a hundred years ago good Romsey ale was as popular a drink with the fair sex as with men, and is becoming so again with the introduction of Golden Ale, a light and refreshing and healthy accompaniment to a meal,' claimed a 1930s brewery guide to the New Forest and the Strong Country. The new brew also took pride of place at the bars of the prestigious Bournemouth Pavilion.

But the golden beer did not neglect its traditional market. In a remarkable 1930s publicity photograph that would be unimaginable today, an elderly man was portrayed holding up a glass of Golden Ale in a pub, alongside a stoppered bottle and a framed poster promoting the sunshine brew. The subliminal message was good health and long life – if you drink a glass or two.

Though the brewery's founder did not fully enjoy this experience. Despite giving his name to what became one of the dominant breweries in southern England, Thomas Strong only owned the eighteenth-century Horsefair brewery for three years from 1883, though he had leased it since 1858. On his death in 1886, David Faber took over the market town business and expanded it rapidly, taking over many local rivals.

The company was badly hit during the Second World War, with sixteen of its houses in Southampton completely destroyed by bombing and many more damaged. Its garages were also requisitioned to store aircraft. But after the conflict it recovered, buying more distant breweries, including Wethered's of Buckinghamshire in 1949 and Mew Langton of the Isle of Wight in 1965.

But by the 1960s the sun was starting to set on the golden glass. Marketing muscle was moving behind the stronger Special Pale Ale and a new keg bitter Barleycorn. When Strong's attempted a cross-Channel export drive to Normandy in 1965, it was these two brews which led the invasion. More ominously, Strong's had since 1955 been linked with Whitbread, who had two seats on the board, and in 1969 the London giant took over, with Strong's beers disappearing from the bars of its 920 pubs spread over eight counties.

Strong's Bitter was rebranded as Trophy, but the Strong name was too strong to die. In 1980 Whitbread Wessex revived the Strong Country legend. CAMRA member Pat O'Neill recalls, 'The local branches received unexpected invitations to the Romsey Brewery to sample test brews of a new, un-named bitter. These samples were excellent, a straw-coloured bitter, highly hopped and notably dry and clean. We went away and welcomed the launch of Strong Country Bitter.'

But the good news soon turned sour, with the Romsey site ceasing to brew the following year. The 'ghost' brand lasted a further sixteen years, being brewed at Whitbread plants in Portsmouth and Cheltenham, and then by Morrell's of Oxford, before being dropped in 1997, though many believed the taste sharply deteriorated once it left the Strong Country.

Even then the Strong spirit would not rest, with the Hampshire Brewery, founded in 1992 in Andover, starting to brew Strong's Best Bitter in 1999 after it moved to Romsey. It closed in 2009, but don't bet against another Strong revival, particularly after another brewery, Flack Manor, opened in Romsey in 2010.

ODD BUT TRUE: A Strong's pub, the Fox & Hounds at Beauworth, used an ancient 12-foot wheel to draw water from a deep well, until it was connected to the mains in the 1950s. Treading inside the wheel, the landlord had to walk 794 yards to haul up an 18-gallon cask.

ODDER BUT TRUE: Even the dead appeared to sing the brewery's praises. A tombstone in Winchester churchyard for Thomas Thatcher, who died in 1764 aged twenty-six, carried the warning, 'Here sleeps in peace a Hampshire Grenadier; Who caught his death by drinking cold, small beer. Soldiers be wise from his untimely fall; And when you're hot, drink Strong or none at all.' The brewery was happy to use the last line of the verse in their marketing, even though Thomas Thatcher died almost a century before Thomas Strong took over the business.

BEER: Yorkshire Stingo
BREWER: Seth Senior & Sons, Shepley, Huddersfield
ALSO KNOWN FOR: Sovereign Stout
BREWERY LOGO: A George IV sovereign
HISTORIC RIVAL: Stingo from Higson's of Liverpool
SIMILAR BREWS TODAY: Yorkshire Stingo (8%) from Samuel Smith of Tadcaster, an annual brew released on Yorkshire Day (1 August)
ILLUSTRATIONS: 141, 195-8

YORKSHIRE STINGO: One of the strangest features of the London brewer Watney's, notorious for its Red Barrel keg beer, was that it also brewed a dark strong ale called Yorkshire Stingo. The beer was even celebrated in bricks and mortar in the capital, as there was a Watney pub called the Yorkshire Stingo on Marylebone Road.

More remarkably still, this had been the brewery tap of the Yorkshire Stingo Brewery in Westminster which Watney's had taken over in 1907 from Woodbridge & Co. This company had registered the Yorkshire Stingo name in 1891, claiming fifty years of use prior to 1875.

But why had the fame of this northern brew travelled so far – and where exactly did it originate? Tracking down the legend takes you to the windswept Pennine village of Shepley, just south of Huddersfield, where in 1829 dry-stone waller Seth Senior started brewing in his cottage. He reputedly borrowed a sovereign to start the business and so called his first pub, The Sovereign, and adopted the coin as his trade mark.

The moorland water was ideal for brewing and he prospered, later helped by his two sons Reuben and James. It was a remarkable brewing family, as another two sons left to establish the famous Barnsley Brewery. Even more remarkably, despite producing a staggeringly strong ale, Seth Senior had a hatred of drunkenness and would not countenance excessive drinking.

In 1865 he took over a nearby rival and built his stores into the hillside so that his beers matured in stable conditions in the days before artificial refrigeration. Was this the cool secret behind Stingo's success? Or was it the water?

When the book *Huddersfield Illustrated* ran a profile of Senior's Highfield Brewery in 1895, the business dominated the village, not only as brewers producing 1,000 barrels a week, but also as maltsters, bottlers, mineral water makers, wine and spirit importers, farmers and grouse moor keepers. It had its own gas works, colliery and railway siding. It was a town within a village, with each group of workers supporting each other.

Thus the miners from their Kirkburton pit were used to build a network of brick culverts to channel the moorland water into a series of reservoirs to feed the brewery and the rest of the village. It was so good that when Tetley's of Leeds suffered from a shortage of water in the mid-1950s, it brought in supplies by tanker from Shepley for brewing.

The author of *Huddersfield Illustrated* certainly thought there was only one Senior beer worth highlighting: 'The inhabitants of the West Riding ... show such a decided and widespread preference for the old Yorkshire stingo of Messrs Senior and Sons ... indeed Senior's stingo is appreciated far beyond the limits of Yorkshire.'

But there were a number of Yorkshire breweries riding on Stingo's reputation. Seth Senior was far from the first, though the brewery claimed to have become the most prominent. Stingo was a local name for strong ale, probably referring to the stinging blow a glass or two could give to the senses. The Oxford Dictionary records it being used as far back as 1635.

Yorkshire beer writer Barrie Pepper found the term in a poem by George Meriton published in York in 1685. It concluded with the lines, 'O Yorkshire, Yorkshire: thy ale is so strong, That it will kill us all, if we stay long.' A hefty draught certainly released the inner poet in drinkers. Anonymous lines from 1697 declared, 'Such stingo, nappy, pure ale they had found; Let's lose no time, said they, but drink a round.' A song, 'A Cup of Old Stingo', appeared in a 1650 book *Merry Drollery Complete*.

Stingo for a time was as symbolic of Yorkshire taste as Yorkshire pudding. And many traded on its powerful name. When Alfred Barnard, author of *The Noted Breweries of Great Britain and Ireland*, visited Tetley's in 1889, he soon found his way to the sample room. After tasting the 'running beers', he was delighted to be handed 'a specimen of Yorkshire Stingo, which we found very luscious, full of body and well flavoured without being heady'.

Some claimed Bradford brewer William Whitaker's Old Brewery, founded in 1757, was the birthplace of Yorkshire Stingo on a commercial scale. Its local rival Hammond's also brewed the devilish drop. When Keith Thomas of Brewlab at the University of Sunderland analysed Hammond's brewing records from 1903, he found its Stingo had an alcohol content of 9.5% (1100 OG). Around 18% glucose was added to the malt mash, but this sweetness was balanced by a sackful of hops to give a rich, complex flavour to savour.

But at Shepley, it appeared, no amount of Stingo could soothe a damaging rift which had appeared in the controlling family. Seth Senior's two grandsons,

Norman and Harold, were said to have stopped speaking to each other. It was a dangerous silence, since one was the head brewer and the other was in charge of bottling. 'The beer passing by pipe from the brewery to the bottling stores was the sole communication between them,' said Hammond's company secretary Anthony Avis.

In 1946 the company shocked its workforce when it decided to sell out to Hammond's, which soon closed the brewery, concentrating local production at its Bentley & Shaw subsidiary in Huddersfield. Stingo lingered for a few years, but the spirit had gone once Hammond's decided to concentrate its marketing efforts behind Bentley & Shaw's strong brew Guards Ale.

Watney's continued brewing its dark stranger from the North for much longer – and to much acclaim. Prince George enjoyed sampling a drop on a surprise royal visit to Watney's Mortlake brewery in 1932. It was viewed as a seasonal beer, ideal for winter drinking. In 1950 it was the first Watney beer to be given national distribution, through a newspaper campaign promoting deliveries of Christmas twelve-bottle boxes of 'rare old Stingo' for the princely sum of £1.

Andrew Campbell in his 1956 *The Book of Beer* commented, 'At the head of the list of the Watney brews stands Stingo, descendant of the famous Yorkshire ale of the barley wine type; semi-sweet and malty, it is a powerful and respected drink.'

Watney's certainly employed no short cuts in its production. A 1954 feature on its cold stores in its house magazine, *The Red Barrel*, revealed that casks of Stingo were matured in No. 15 cellar at Mortlake for at least ten to twelve months before bottling, with the large barrels regularly rolled by hand. It was by far its most expensive bottled beer, costing 1/6d for a nip-size (third of a pint) bottle in April, 1956, the same as a whole pint of bitter. It had an original gravity around 1080 (8% alcohol).

In the 1980s bottles were even being exported to the USA under the slogan 'A Fistful of Flavour' before Watney's pulled out of brewing in 1990. Its London brewery at Mortlake was later sold to American brewer Anheuser-Busch to brew a very different beer – Budweiser.

ODD BUT TRUE: When Hammond's took over Seth Senior in 1946, it also inherited a land war. Huddersfield Corporation was building its own reservoirs and wanted to take over a Senior's pub, The Isle of Skye, on the top of the moor. The legal battle had been raging since the 1930s and only in 1958 did Hammond's agree to sell – on condition it could erect a sign near the demolished pub on the Holmfirth road directing travellers to the nearest Hammond's inn. The sign stood for twelve years.

WALES

BEER: Crown SBB
BREWER: South Wales and Monmouthshire United Clubs Brewery, Pontyclun
ALSO KNOWN FOR: CPA, Brown Bracer and Triple Crown
BREWERY LOGO: A crown
HISTORIC RIVAL: Buckley's Best Bitter from Llanelli
SIMILAR BREWS TODAY: Welsh Gold from Bullmastiff Brewery of Cardiff
ILLUSTRATIONS: 142, 143, 145, 199-201

CROWN SBB: When CAMRA's national research officer Danny Blyth was sent to South Wales in 1983 to investigate the region's clubs' brewery, he didn't know what to expect, as its beers were rarely seen outside club bars. 'They'll probably be nae special,' grumbled the Scotsman. When he returned he had a problem – how to rearrange his top division of Britain's best beers.

He had been converted at the end of the road to Pontyclun by his first taste of Crown SBB, while drinking in the sample room. 'I was left with a very deep impression ... of a crew of brewery workers whose faith in the pint in their hands I have not heard matched anywhere,' he reported.

The Crown Brewery had always generated deep affection – as it was one of the few breweries in Britain owned by its drinkers. And the quality of SBB (Special Best Bitter) was not only praised by locals. In 1964 the brewery's premium draught beer had won the Challenge Cup for cask beer at the Brewers' Exhibition in London, in competition with 379 entries. The original founders of the brewery would not have dreamed of such a crowning achievement. They just wanted a reliable supply of good beer at a fair price.

The venture had sprung out of a bitter dispute between the region's commercial breweries and their club customers during the First World War. With harsh government restrictions limiting the amount of beer produced, the breweries supplied their own pubs first. And what beer did trickle through to the clubs was low in strength and high in cost. The clubs were not impressed by the product, the price or the poor service. They vowed to act once the war was over. And they didn't hang about.

In 1919 the clubs bought Jenkins' Crown Brewery at Pontyclun for £25,000. It provided a ready-made solution as it was ideally situated at the gateway to the mining Valleys, where it already supplied working men's clubs with Crown Pale Ale and XXXX dark mild. It was to be run by the CIU clubs as the South Wales and Monmouthshire United Clubs Brewery, with clubs receiving a discount on the price of beer depending on their shareholding, as well as bonuses on the number of barrels bought. The drinkers were in the driving seat.

The established brewers were scornful and ridiculed the move. 'The whole scheme seems to be plastered with ineptitude,' pronounced *The Brewers' Journal* in a lengthy editorial in July 1919. Forty-five years later the same trade magazine was to sponsor the prestigious cup won by Crown. The industry was alarmed because clubs breweries were not only appearing in South Wales but also across Britain, notably in the industrial Midlands and North of England. The brewers feared that their profitable businesses would face cut-price competition. And they were right to be concerned.

By the Second World War the Pontyclun brewery's annual production had reached almost 30,000 barrels, three times the original output, and the old plant was creaking at the seams. After the conflict a larger £260,000 brewery was built behind the old one, with substantial financial help from the Northern Clubs Federation Brewery of Newcastle. It finally opened in 1954 and ushered in a decade of success.

That year production topped 50,000 barrels and the new plant allowed the brewery to introduce new beers, though the clubs, always keen on low prices, were not immediately eager for a premium beer selling at 1s 4d a pint when SBB was launched in 1958. Only eleven clubs placed an order for a total of fourteen barrels. On such slim hopes was a champion born. After its success in 1964, the best bitter (3.7%) with a marked hoppy flavour went on to account for a third of production, remarkably still delivered in wooden casks.

The co-operative movement had silenced its critics, with clubs benefiting from the large bonuses. In the five years to 1964, £790,000 was given back to members, and much more was provided in loans to fund improvements to premises. As the firm's slogan claimed, 'Loyalty Pays'.

But that loyalty was stretched to the limit as aggressive brewing combines replaced old family firms. Led by Welsh Brewers (Bass) and Whitbread in South Wales, they launched heavily-promoted keg beers. In response the clubs brewery introduced its own tank and keg beers like Crown Keg and Great Western, but they struggled to compete.

It's interesting to note how the processed beers were viewed. When creating Great Western in 1976, the brewers were instructed to produce a brew 'of a bland acceptable nature, taking all necessary steps to eliminate the existing tangy, bitter palate of our existing beers'. The board did not want a distinctive beer like SBB.

The same year it smartened up to its image by formally dropping its cumbersome South Wales and Monmouthshire United Clubs Brewery title for the snappier Crown name. As other clubs breweries in England collapsed, it tried to expand into the West Midlands, but the move proved too costly to sustain. Instead it began to supply pubs, its cask beers still in wooden barrels appealing to real ale drinkers. In 1975 when CAMRA opened one of its first pubs, the Old Fox in Bristol, hand-pumped SBB was featured on the bar.

Crown was losing its clubs identity. In 1975 its application to join the once hostile South Wales Brewers' Association was accepted. The clubs company had come in from the cold, and began building its own pub estate in the 1980s and even opening a depot in London. In 1988 it completed this switch to a more traditional brewing company when, backed by Guinness, it took over the troubled Buckley's Brewery of Llanelli with 130 pubs. A new company, Crown Buckley, was formed.

The surprise merger spelled the end of brewing at Pontyclun, with Buckley's Llanelli plant providing the beer. Only packaging was carried out at the old clubs site, though the brewing vessels remained in place. A visitor later recalled that 'the Pontyclun plant has the air of a ghost brewery, even two years after its closure. White brewers' coats still hang on the pegs where they were left. "Grains in the mash tun are not to be touched until 1 p.m." says a dusty notice. They remain untouched.' Buckley's Best Bitter led Crown Buckley's sales drive with SBB left in the shadows.

But it proved a costly gamble that did not pay off as sales plunged in the recession. Late in 1990 Guinness stepped in and took control, as the banks threatened to pull the plug.

The new management team under Mike Salter was perplexed by some of the goings-on at the club site. On one of his first mornings, he noticed a coach pull up and a party tumble out into 'The Hatch', a room where staff enjoyed free beer. On going to investigate he discovered the visitors helping themselves. It seemed club outings regularly called at the plant on their way to the races. He closed The Hatch.

Gradually they turned trade around, launching a new premium cask beer Reverend James in 1991, named after one of the founders of Buckley's Brewery. In 1993 the team invested in a management buyout of the business. But the venture did not last long. In 1997 they sold up to Brain's of Cardiff. Brain's closed Buckley's Brewery the next year, followed by the Pontyclun plant, with the old clubs site cleared for housing in 2000. SBB disappeared from the bar to leave just a few tasty memories of a time when the customer really was king.

ODD BUT TRUE: Crown's low-gravity keg beer Brenin Bitter was originally called Same Again. The strange name did not last long.

BEER: Five Five
BREWER: William Hancock of Newport, Cardiff and Swansea
ALSO KNOWN FOR: Amber Ale, Nut Brown and HB
BREWERY LOGO: Initially a phoenix but later John Bull
HISTORIC RIVAL: Brain's bottled IPA (1046) from Cardiff
SIMILAR BREWS TODAY: Celt Bronze (1046) from the Celt Experience, Caerphilly
ILLUSTRATIONS: 144, 146, 202-4

FIVE FIVE: In Britain less than forty years ago, drinkers were not given any information about the strength of beers. The industry argued that if the details were revealed, many would gravitate to the more potent brews, leading to drunkenness.

Beer drinkers could not be trusted to drink sensibly, only insensibly. It was best to leave them in ignorance. In reality the brewers did not want people to know the truth – that many beers after the Second World War were astonishingly weak, even when they claimed to be strong.

Take the case of William Hancock, once the brewing giant of South Wales, which was not only a prime offender, but later tried to make amends by producing a strong ale with its strength highlighted in its name – Five Five. It became a number to savour for some Welsh drinkers, after decades of anaemic brews.

William Hancock, a brewer from Wiveliscombe in Somerset, had founded the Welsh business in 1883 when he bought the Bute Dock Brewery in Cardiff, followed the next year by the Anchor Brewery in Newport. In 1887 a separate company was formed with a share capital of £100,000 and many more breweries were swept up, including the West End Brewery in Swansea in 1890. Brewing in Cardiff was concentrated at the County Brewery in Crawshay Street after it was bought in 1894. The Hancock's name covered the coast, promoted after 1926 by a jovial John Bull figure holding up a glass. But what exactly was in that pot of beer?

The ales produced across South Wales were influenced by two major factors. First was the strength of the temperance movement. The second was the constant need to brew enough beer to meet demand in a rapidly expanding industrial region. This combination meant that the beers tended to be weaker than in England. In 1894, when the average original gravity of mild across the UK was above 1050 (more than 5% alcohol), Hancock's popular XX was 1043. By 1905 it had fallen to 1040 (4%). It remained at this level until 1915, before the death of beer's body in the First World War.

By the end of the conflict the quality of XX had been so degraded that Hancock's dropped the beer. Its basic brews became XPA (1032) and PA (1040). Unlike Cardiff rivals Brain's, who were famous for their Dark, Hancock's were known for their draught pale ales. The Second World War and the rationing which followed torpedoed the surviving strength of these brews below the waterline. XPA plunged to 1030 (3%) and PA was barely stronger at 1032. Draught mild's reputation never fully recovered. It was increasingly viewed as a wishy-washy beer and drinkers began to switch to bitter. Hancock's HB had only fallen to 1039 by 1955. Others turned to more reliable bottled beers – but they were in for a shock.

Many bottled beers had also lost their bottle. Nut Brown Ale, launched as a premium rich brown ale in 1928, had sunk from 1048 to 1033 by 1960. More staggering was Hancock's Strong Ale, which defied the Trades Descriptions Act with a gravity of 1030 (3%). In 1960, bottled Strong Ale was the brewery's weakest beer. It was only strong on deception. There was nothing new about this misleading marketing. It was widespread in the industry. Rival brewer Buckley's of Llanelli even took a sly dig at this practice in the late 1920s by advertising its brew as 'The Strong Ale that IS Strong!'

Hancock's always liked to present a reassuring olde worlde image, backed up by its smart teams of traditional grey horses. But behind the façade of solid tradition, its ales were always altering. This is true of all breweries, but we know more facts about Hancock's because after Bass Charrington's takeover in 1968, Norman Bridgwater, the quality control manager for Bass Production Wales, wrote a report detailing how the beer styles and strengths had been transformed down the decades. In its pages, there was no longer any hiding place for Hancock's Strong Ale.

But they also reveal a determined attempt to launch a genuine strong ale after the Second World War. And one which openly declared its strength for all to see, even if this honest claim soon started to slip. Called Five Five, with an original gravity of 1055, this strong bottled pale ale was part of a drive to develop an export trade, but proved popular at home with drinkers eager for a beer with real body, despite its strength soon being slightly lowered to 1048.

But Hancock's biggest headache came from the name. On the initial label, the figures 55 stood out, so drinkers asked for Fifty Five. The brewery tried to nudge them towards the correct title by adding a dash between the figures, but with little success. Eventually they dropped the numbers and just spelt out Five Five. There was also briefly a Seven Seven export stout, but Five Five lasted longer. It became the company's new flagship beer in distinctive, dumpy bottles – along with a processed mild.

Hancock's in 1964 introduced a keg version of its popular PA called Allbright, which soon shone in many Welsh pubs and clubs. There was also a keg version of HB called Barleybrite, served from a large plastic wheatsheaf on the bar. Unusually, it used nitrogen rather than carbon-dioxide for dispense, giving the beer a creamy texture.

After the Bass Charrington takeover, the beer range was rationalised. Five Five disappeared along with Barleybrite. The John Bull figure soon only still lifted his glass on pump clips for HB. But Allbright continued to shine, the name being displayed on the towering brewery chimney next to Cardiff Central railway station. In the 1990s, Bass claimed it accounted for a staggering one in five pints of ale drunk in South Wales. Sales were helped by it now being branded a bitter.

While the Swansea brewery had closed in 1969 after the takeover, the old Hancock's brewery in Cardiff continued to steam away until 1999, when Bass decided to shut it. But there was a saviour waiting nearby. Cardiff brewers Brain's bought the brewery and moved in from its cramped city centre site in St Mary Street. Along with its own beers, Brain's now brews Hancock's HB under licence at Hancock's early home in Crawshay Street. John Bull lives on. But there was no final throw of the dice for Five Five. Its number had long been up.

ODD BUT TRUE: One of William Hancock's sons, Frank, who came over from Somerset to Cardiff to help run the new company, became a Welsh rugby legend, leading Cardiff in their near-invincible season in 1885–6, and also captaining Wales.

BEER: Rhymney PMA
BREWER: Andrew Buchan's Breweries, Rhymney, Monmouthshire
ALSO KNOWN FOR: Hobby Horse and King's Ale
BREWERY LOGO: A huntsman on a barrel-bodied horse
HISTORIC RIVAL: Hancock's PA from Cardiff, later called Allbright in keg form
ILLUSTRATIONS: 147, 148, 205

RHYMNEY PMA: Henry Holder, who was a brewer at Rhymney from 1962 until 1975, recalled the stark figures. 'We brewed Golden Hop Bitter (GHB), a pale bitter at 1036 and Pale Mild Ale (PMA), a lager-coloured mild, at 1030 [original gravity]. The weekly production of these beers was 250 barrels of GHB and 1,750 barrels of PMA.'

The pale mild, despite its weak strength (3% alcohol), totally dominated production. The reason was simple, as explained in the company's 1959 guidebook to its pubs *Where the Rhymney Hobby Horse Roams*: 'For two centuries the Valleys of the famous South Wales coalfield have been the battlefield where industry has fought nature to a standstill.' It added, 'Where hard physical work and heat brought sweat to the brow, and the loss of moisture and salt in the body had to be replaced, beer in large quantities had to be made available.'

PMA was just the right beer to knock back after a day at the coal face or near the blast furnace. Henry Holder recalled that one club in Tredegar in the early 1960s took 17 hogsheads (huge 54-gallon casks) of PMA – not once but twice a week. That's more than fifty 36-gallon barrels every seven days. It sold at 1s 3d a pint. The sheer difficulty of handling such amounts led Rhymney to introduce tank beer, delivered by road tankers which piped the mild direct into large cellar tanks.

More exalted Rhymney brews like the powerful bottled King's Ale, first introduced for Edward VII's coronation in 1902, might be promoted as 'The Wine of the Valleys', but the beer for everyday drinking was mild. The wider range of 'Rhymney' bottled beers was no longer brewed in the Valleys, but at the firm's sister plant, Crosswell's of Cardiff. Draught PMA, or Amber as it was also called, reigned supreme at Rhymney. Some brews had added caramel to produce a darker mild.

The brewery's roots were sunk as deep as a pit shaft into local industry. It had been established in 1839 by the Rhymney Iron Company to slake its workers' thirsts, and was managed by a stern Scotsman Andrew Buchan, who also oversaw the extensive company shop. Despite running the brewery, he was a keen temperance advocate and would not employ heavy drinkers. Out of this conflict of interests developed less intoxicating beers. Its basic brew was XX mild. It proved a recipe for success.

By Buchan's death in 1870, the brewery was considered the largest in South Wales, dominating the bottom of the valley alongside the railway line. It had grown to overshadow the ironworks, which closed in 1890. And in 1929 the brewery broke free of its iron links when it merged with Griffiths Brothers brewery of Blaina to form Andrew Buchan's Breweries.

A spurt of acquisitions followed, the first being significant for allowing a familiar figure to ride into view. When Pritchard's Western Valleys Brewery in Crumlin was taken over in 1930, Rhymney also inherited its hobby horse trademark, showing a huntsman astride a galloping barrel-bodied nag. Buchan quickly saddled up the charismatic emblem for its own use.

In 1936 two larger scalps were seized – the last major concern in Merthyr Tydfil, David Williams' Taff Vale Brewery, and Crosswell's Cardiff Brewery. Others followed. The hobby horse was leaping into a bigger brewing league, owning more than 350 pubs. But after the war, while it was big enough to attract attention from prowling predators, it was not large enough to ward off their advances. So in 1951 it became the first brewery to shelter under what became known as the Whitbread umbrella, allowing the London brewer to take a share stake and seats on the board in return for protection.

In 1958 an accomplished rider leaped into the hobby horse saddle when the Olympic showjumper Colonel Harry Llewellyn became chairman, spurring the nag into a final gallop. He changed the company name to Rhymney Breweries, but the Valleys site was becoming a backwater of the business, being dismissed in a report as 'an old-fashioned brewery on the side of a hill'. New brands like a Hobby Horse keg beer flowed from Crosswell's in Cardiff, as did more ambitious brews like Ski Lager and Tivoli 'the modern ale for modern women'. Rhymney was further sidelined with the takeover of the Ely Brewery in Cardiff in 1959. The major merger meant the company now owned 730 pubs, and virtually a new brewery was built on Crosswell's Cardiff site in 1962 to handle production.

But there was one major flaw in Rhymney's Whitbread umbrella – it didn't protect you from Whitbread with its 30% share stake. And in 1966 the London giant stepped in and took control when Rhymney was struggling to finance all its plans. An angry shareholder described it as 'a marriage with every sign of a shotgun in the background'. The hobby horse was hobbled and soon replaced by Whitbread's logo, the hind's head.

Whitbread Trophy and Tankard now took pride of place at the bar. But PMA continued to be brewed at Rhymney until the brewery closed in 1978, despite an attempt by student unions in the region, backed by local MP Michael Foot, to form a co-operative to run the brewery to supply college bars. But PMA didn't then completely vanish, as a low-gravity Welsh Bitter, based on the light mild, was brewed at the group's giant Magor complex alongside the M4 for Whitbread Wales.

Nor did the Rhymney name and hobby horse disappear into the sunset. In 2005 local businessman Steve Evans began brewing in Dowlais under the Rhymney name, later adopting the hobby horse as his logo. In 2012 he moved to a new site in Blaenavon. Fittingly it lies between the town's historic ironworks and the Big Pit tourist attraction. Rhymney is surrounded by industry again. But Steve Evans could not reawaken the area's taste for light mild. That had died along with the mines.

ODD BUT TRUE: In 1936 King Edward VIII visited Rhymney's old company shop, which was being used for work projects, to meet the unemployed. It was his last public appearance before he abdicated.

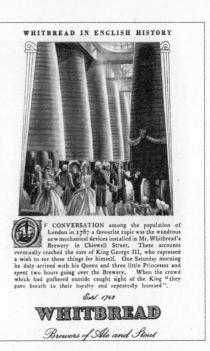

Above left: 166. An 1873 painting of Whitbread's gloomy Old Vat House in Chiswell Street captures the vast size of the vessels. Some were as high as 38 feet. If they gave way, a tidal wave of beer was let loose (see pages 84–6).

Above right: 167. The major London brewers used their towering vats to impress eminent visitors. Whitbread was still trading on this past in an advert in 1949.

168. An engraving of Meux's Brewery in 1830 from *Old and New London* (see pages 84–86).

Above left: 169. Castle in the air – Nimmo's Schloss Lager did not last long (see page 88).

Above right: 170. Dutton's claimed OBJ was a 'genuine old English ale' (see pages 91–3).

Above left: 171. OBJ was widely promoted across the North of England (see pages 91–3).

Above right: 172. Beasley's also carried a heavy drop of OBJ in the South East of England (see pages 93–4).

173. Old Ram butted Ramsden's
to national prominence in 1932
(see pages 94–6).

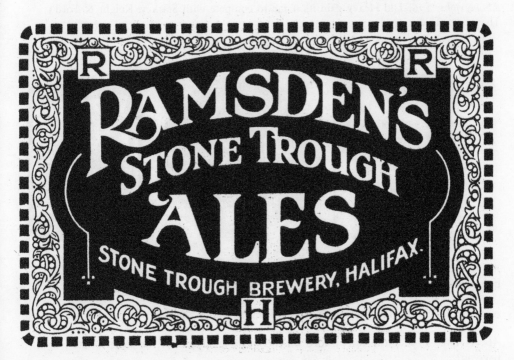

174. Ramsden's advertised its beer as 'Stone Trough Ales' (see pages 94–6).

Above left: 175. Plymouth's Regent Brewery was better known for its pale ales, as in this 1952 advert for No. 1 IPA (see pages 96–7).

Above right: 176. Did Heavy gain its name to compete with Starkey, Knight & Ford's Tivvy from Tiverton? (See pages 96–7.)

Above left: 177. Plymouth was a highly traditional brewery, taking pride in its wooden barrels (see page 97).

Above middle: 178. The alarm bells were ringing at Phipps (see pages 98–9).

Above right: 179. 'Little Rat' traded on the wartime success of the Desert Rats (see page 99).

Above left: 180. Brothers Alaric and Quentin Neville revived the famous brew in 2009 (see page 99).

Above right: 181. NBC's Jumbo Stout was held up above Ratliffe's Stout after the merger (see page 99).

182. The Cornish brewery made an extravagant early claim to brew 'The World's Stout' (see page 100).

Above left: 183. Devenish boasted five Royal Warrants for its Weymouth beers (see pages 100–2).

Above right: 184. The Commemoration brew was probably based on Style & Winch's potent Barley Wine (see pages 102–4).

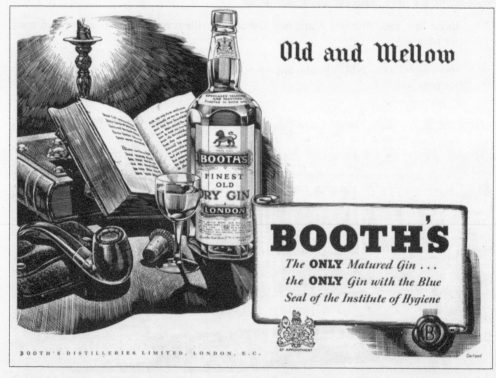

185. Booth's Gin distillery used the original trade mark of the Royal Brewery – a red lion (see pages 102–4).

Above left: 186. Barclay's Brewery adopted Dr Johnson as the brewery trade mark and featured him on its Russian Imperial Stout labels, shown in this 1934 advert.

Above right: 187. Barclay's also produced a bottled Double Brown Stout for the home market, as advertised on this pottery bar stand (see pages 104–6).

188. A huge mirror advertising Barclay's 'Imperial Stout and matchless Porter' took pride of place at the reopening of The Champion pub off Oxford Street in 1955.

189. Shipstone's star ales were promoted by cartoon character Ivor Thirst in the 1950s (see pages 106–8).

190. A sketch of the grand brewery dominated Shipstone's business letters.

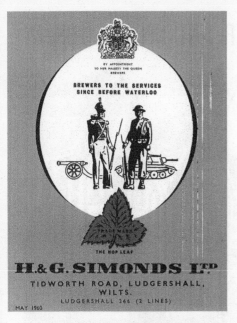

Above left: 191. Simonds was still promoting its military links on the cover of its price lists in 1960 (see pages 109–11).

Above right: 192. Farson's Hop Leaf label. In 1929 Simonds merged its Maltese agency with local brewers Farson's, so its Hop Leaf Pale Ale could be brewed on the island (see page 110).

193. Simonds was one of the early pioneers of canned beer in Britain (see pages 109–11).

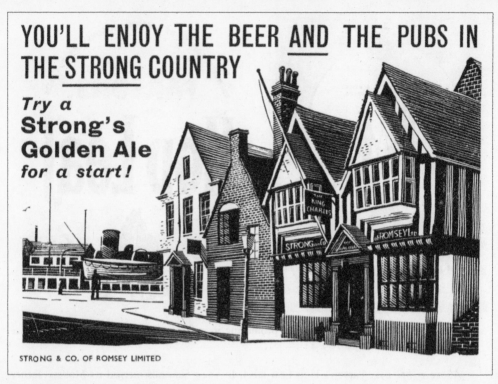

194. Golden Ale missed out on Strong's export drive in 1965 (see pages 111–13).

Above left: 195. Stinging brew – Hammond's Yorkshire Stingo had a strength of 9.5% in 1903 (see page 114).

Above right: 196. Seth's 'Fine Ales' disappeared after the Hammond's takeover in 1946 (see pages 113–15).

197. Casks of Stingo were matured at Watney's Mortlake Brewery by the Thames for at least ten to twelve months (see pages 113–15).

Above left: 198. Watney's Stingo had a muscular alcohol strength of around 8%.

Above right: 199. 'Loyalty Pays' – as the Clubs Brewery paid members bonuses on the amount of beer bought (see pages 116–18).

Right: 200. After SBB's crowning achievement in 1964, it went on to account for a third of sales.

201. The new clubs brewery opened in 1954 followed by the introduction of tank beer in 1963 (see pages 116–18).

Above left: 202. Five Five poster. Five Five brought lost strength back to Hancock's beer (see pages 118–20).

Above right: 203. Hancock's HB is now back home, brewed in the old Hancock's Brewery in Cardiff.

204. The spotlight was on Hancock's 55 after 1945 (see pages 118–20).

205. Rhymney had to battle against a strong temperance movement in the chapels. It hit back in 1922 with this Bateman cartoon (*above left*) of a soft drinks saloon for miners (Picture: National Museum of Wales) (see pages 121–2).

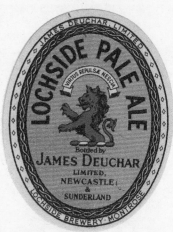

Above left: 206. Dark Lager was the first beer brewed by Wrexham in 1883.

Above middle: 207. Wrexham liked to claim it was the oldest lager brewery in the UK, as in this 1905 advert. Tennent's of Glasgow strongly disagreed (see pages 141–3).

Above right: 208. James Deuchar made a fortune in North East England (see pages 146–8).

209. Scotch on the rocks – only months after this poster was produced in 1898, the Pattisons' company was sunk (see pages 147–8).

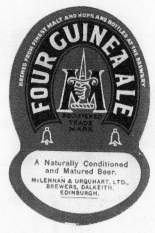

Above left: 210. Lochside Export was popular on Tyneside in the 1950s (see pages 146–8).

Above right: 211. McLennan & Urquart of Dalkeith produced a Four Guinea Ale (see page 149).

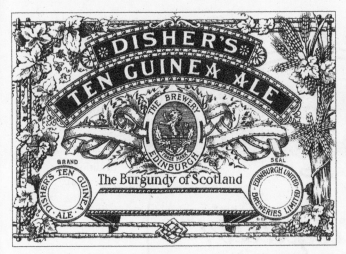

Above left: 212. The original elaborate gold label of Disher's Ten Guinea (Label: Andrew Cunningham) (see pages 148–50).

Above right: 213. Edinburgh United and Disher's were once two of Scotland's most prominent brewing names.

Traquair
House Ale

A potent liquor brewed by the Laird in the
ancient Brew House of the Oldest
Inhabited House in Scotland.

9⅔ fl.oz. 275 mls. BOTTLED AT
BELHAVEN BREWERY, DUNBAR

ORIGINAL GRAVITY 1073-1080°

*Above and
left:* 214 &
215. Peter
Maxwell
Stuart's
revived
Traquair
House Ale
is in the
'Wee Heavy'
tradition (see
page 149).

Above left: 216. Maclay's 'Most Nourishing and Strengthening' Oatmalt Stout proudly displays its 1894 medal on its early label.

Above right: 217. Oatmalt Stout became one of Maclay's flagship beers (see pages 151–3).

218. In 1919, as the USA embraced Prohibition, George Younger launched non-alcoholic Pony Beer (see page 154).

219. No. 3 was Younger's leading beer in London, in bottle or on draught (see pages 155–8).

220. William Younger celebrated its anniversary in 1949 with Double Century, which was so popular it became a regular part of the beer range (see page 157).

BEER: Wrexham Dark Lager
BREWER: Wrexham Lager Beer Company, North Wales
ALSO KNOWN FOR: Wrexham Pilsener and Four Aces
BREWERY LOGO: The Ace of Clubs and later the original Bavarian-style brewery buildings
HISTORIC RIVAL: Barclay's Dark Lager
SIMILAR BREWS TODAY: Black Lager (4.6%) from Zerodegrees of Cardiff
ILLUSTRATIONS: 149-51, 206, 207

WREXHAM DARK LAGER: When British drinkers ask for a lager they expect to see a glass of golden beer with a foaming white head. But originally many lagers were almost as black as stout. And the first beer to pour out of the Wrexham brewery, which claimed to be the oldest lager brewer in the UK, was definitely a dark drop.

A group of Manchester businessmen, led by German and Czech immigrants, formed the company in 1881 as they saw a market for lager in Britain and its colonies. They chose Wrexham as the site for the brewery because of the town's reputation as a brewing centre. Engineers from Austria drew up the plans for the plant on St Mark's Road, where the water was as soft as Pilsen, the Czech town which had pioneered pale lager forty years before.

By the end of 1883 the brewery had been built with six underground cellars dug into the hillside containing 200 maturation vessels. An ice-making machine was intended to chill the cellars like a freezing continental winter. Then their golden dreams were shattered. The ice-maker couldn't cope with mild, wet Wales. Its failure meant only a dark Bavarian-style lager could be produced. Worse, local drinkers ignored the strange new brew in town. Then a formidable figure came to the rescue.

Manufacturing chemist Robert Graesser joined the board in 1886. An innovator, he introduced mechanical refrigeration to cool the cellars, allowing light lagers to be produced. But sales were still small and scattered as far as Edinburgh and Dublin, despite winning medals at exhibitions. Wrexham Lager was even marketed as a temperance drink, as it was weaker than the strong British ales of the time. 'When more generally known and consumed, it will diminish intoxication and do more for the temperance cause than all the efforts of the total abstainers,' it claimed. But this weak market could not support the business. In 1892 the company went into liquidation.

But Robert Graesser was not one to give up. He bought the firm and looked abroad for better sales, producing bottled lagers under a variety of brands for the many British trading companies of the period. Wrexham was also a major garrison town and he determined to follow the flag around the Empire. The brewery's Ace of Clubs trademark soon found itself dealt into some desperate battles.

A letter dated 21 September 1898, from a Sergeant Major serving in the Sudan, read, 'Gentlemen, I enclose herewith one of your labels which was taken off a bottle found in the grounds of Gordon's Palace at Khartoum ... just to let you know how far your famous Wrexham Lager Beer can be had.' The brewery was developing a following in global hot-spots. By the turn of the century 80% of production was for export.

Robert Graesser found another market in 1904 when he travelled to America on the White Star liner SS *Baltic* and insisted on taking a supply of draught dark lager with him. The beer survived the voyage so well that the shipping line decided to stock it. A lucrative business supplying cruise liners had set sail.

The family firm's trade and expertise in producing light and dark lagers began to attract attention within the brewing industry. English giants Barclay Perkins made an offer for the company just before the First World War – on condition that Edgar Graesser, who had taken over running the brewery after the death of his father in 1911, remained at the helm. The family turned down the bid and Barclays brewed its own light and dark lagers in London in 1921 instead.

Wrexham Lager was also beginning to build a local following. Miners developed a taste for the unfiltered dark lager, rich in malt extract. They would call in at the brewery and pay a penny a pint more for a drop most today would send straight back to the bar – cloudy beer from the bottom of the barrel, specially sold in swing-top bottles, believing that with its high yeast content they were receiving a meal as well as a drink.

The lagers were becoming so popular that the town's local ale brewers banded together to keep the beers out of their bars. In response in 1922 Wrexham Lager bought its first pub, the Cross Foxes in Abbot Street. It became the first in Britain to serve chilled draught lager, the pipes running through lead-lined boxes packed with ice from the brewery's refrigeration plant. Trade in the pub frothed up to thirty barrels a week.

Wrexham issued a 'What is Lager?' leaflet to explain 'The Champagne of Beers' to local drinkers: 'You do not drink new wines, so why drink new beer? Lager beer means stored beer, so called because true lager is stored for three months before it leaves the brewery. It matures and becomes round in flavour.'

Export trade through Liverpool was also booming. Whole trains of covered wagons had to be used to supply major liners like the RMS *Mauretania* with 1,800 small casks. The brewery was ideally sited right next to the railway line, with its own siding.

There was just one major problem – the beer was too good. Brewing perfectionist Edgar Graesser, who had studied extensively in Germany, insisted on maintaining the German beer purity law, the *Reinheitsgebot*, and the original gravity of the lager at 1052 despite the strength of most British beers having declined considerably. Rivals like Barclay's began to produce weaker, cheaper lagers and steal Wrexham's trade.

In response Edgar Graesser rolled out a Club Lager at 1045 gravity but he was never proud of it. On one occasion he visited London brewery Meux, which was selling Club Lager in its pubs, and said he would prefer to supply the proper Wrexham Pilsner. Meux's managing director responded, 'Mr Graesser, we hate lager like a devil hates holy water. For God's sake don't offer us a better lager. I wish it were so poor that everyone coming into our houses would reject it and order our Treble Gold instead.'

In 1938 Wrexham Lager made a major breakthrough into the local trade when it bought the twenty-three pubs of Beirne's on the closure of the Albion Brewery. After fifty-five years of pouring around the globe, the Ace of Clubs lagers at last flowed freely in their home town. But it was to prove a brief moment of success.

The Second World War blew away Wrexham's export and liner trade. Thousands of casks were lost at sea. And Edgar Graesser left the company after another row over lager quality. With the brewing plant run down and the cost of re-equipping too great, in 1949 the company sold out to Burton brewers Ind Coope & Allsopp.

The takeover spelled the end for Wrexham Dark. It was dropped in 1952. Though Ind Coope invested heavily in the brewery, it used it to brew national brands like Skol and later foreign lagers like Löwenbräu of Munich. It regarded the light Wrexham Lager, reduced to 3.4% alcohol, as a local nuisance and did little to promote it, selling the Ace of Clubs trademark to the Northern Clubs Federation Brewery of Newcastle in 1963.

But Wrexham would not die, still being served in almost 400 pubs and clubs. In 1978 the Allied Breweries group bowed to local pressure, reviving the Wrexham Lager Brewery Company name and adopting a logo showing the old brewery buildings. In 1982 Wrexham marked its centenary by brewing and bottling its dark lager again. A year later it even briefly test-marketed a hand-pulled cask lager called Gold Cross.

But the dreams of a Wrexham revival did not last. In 1992 Allied merged with Danish giants Carlsberg, putting the future of the Wrexham plant in doubt. It finally closed in 2000, with another brew of the delicious Dark (5%) marking the black day. Production of 'Wrexham' Lager was briefly moved to Thwaites of Blackburn, then Tetley's of Leeds, before ending in 2003.

In 2001 a consortium of local businessmen, led by former Wrexham Lager managing director David Priestley, had tried to buy the brand and brew in the former Cambrian Brewery in Wrexham, but the talks broke down. Later Clwyd South MP Martyn Jones did secure the brand, and in 2011 the Roberts family, who run a wholesale distributors business in Wrexham, opened a new brewery using German plant in St George's Crescent. The brewery manager was Ian Dale, previously Wrexham's head brewer. Wrexham Lager was back.

ODD BUT TRUE: Some drinkers went to enormous lengths to catch a drop of the dark lager. Crates used to be stacked in the bottling room just below a hole in the wall. It was noted that the top bottles often went missing. Eventually two men were caught fishing through the hole with a noose on a line trying to snare a bottle.

SCOTLAND

BEER: Aitken's Sparkling Ale
BREWER: James Aitken of Falkirk, founded in 1740 by John Aitken
ALSO KNOWN FOR: Aitken's Export, Strong Ale, 90/- and Stout
BREWERY LOGO: A large letter A, but also used a caged tiger with the word Aitkens
in stripes along its body. Sometimes linked with the slogan 'Strength behind bars'.
HISTORIC RIVAL: McEwan's Pale Ale from Edinburgh
SIMILAR BREWS TODAY: Raj IPA from the Tryst Brewery of Larbert, Stirlingshire
ILLUSTRATIONS: 152-4

AITKEN'S SPARKLING ALE: James Aitken was a man with a mission, handed
down through his family since 1740. He was a brewer who preached the gospel of
'temperance' – moderate drinking. And he didn't mince his words.

> To spread the cause of temperance – that is, real temperance – you must teach the
> public to appreciate wholesome, nourishing, pure beer of the type turned out in
> extensive and ever-growing quantity by this house. Once a man has tasted this
> liquor, he will not thereafter be satisfied with the heavy, thirst-provoking ales, or
> thin, wishy-washy foreign lagers that are unfortunately so often met with today.

He was expounding on 'Pure Beer for Club and Service Men' in the *War Office Times
and Naval Review* in 1908, eight years after his company had built 'a wonderful new
brewery' in Falkirk with the emphasis on cleanliness and 'pure air, pure materials and
perfect plant'. He insisted on the best Scottish, English and African barley and Kentish
hops (German and Californian hops he dismissed as giving an 'oniony flavour').

He produced all-malt beers, using malt from Aitken's own substantial maltings
at nearby Linlithgow, and water from two artesian wells sunk into an underground
loch. 'The outcome is beer with perfect flavour, good body and exceptional
stimulating and nutritive properties – liquor of the type on which the battles of the
past have been fought – and won.'

He was fighting on two fronts. On the one hand he was attacking brewers
who used poorer quality malt and hops and other ingredients to produce cheaper
beers. The question of quality was a burning issue. Only a few years before arsenic
contamination had killed hundreds of beer drinkers in North West England. At

the same time he was battling a powerful anti-alcohol movement which demanded total prohibition.

He was keen to advocate a light bitter beer for the armed forces. Aitken's had begun to specialise in pale ales early in the 19th century, well ahead of most breweries in Britain. They took pride in innovation, being the first Scottish brewers to bottle at the brewery. In 1830 they had taken out a patent for a 'carbonic acid gas plant' to preserve bottled beer. No expense was spared to ensure quality. Only new bottles direct from the manufacturer were used, and even then they were thoroughly washed and rinsed. An early beam engine had been installed in the 1830s to power cask washing.

Besides major trade in India and exports as far as Newfoundland and Hong Kong, the company had a high profile in Australia. A glance at the many medals won by its beers demonstrate its proud progress down under – Sydney (1879), Melbourne (1880), Adelaide (1887), Melbourne (1888) and Brisbane (1897). When Alfred Barnard visited the Falkirk brewery in 1887 for his work *Noted Breweries of Great Britain and Ireland*, he claimed, 'It is not surprising that a product so excellent as Aitken's beer ... should have become the standard drink in Australia and the colonies.'

Their overseas market was extensive, including sales under the Peacock brand in Burma and the 'Nun Nicer' label featuring a demure nun in a garland of hops. 'Their trade is principally export,' noted Barnard, foreign sales having 'rapidly increased' in the last fifty years. This was despite significant home trade, with offices and stores in Glasgow. A fleet of their own barges delivered the beer by canal as well as the brewery having its own railway siding. The export stores and bottling plant were 'the most extensive and important on the [five-acre] site'.

And beer was not Aitken's only export to Australia. When the brewery produced an embossed brochure in 1940 to celebrate '200 years of progress', it boasted, 'The company has been famous the world over for its beer and some say that it was Aitken's who taught the Australians how to brew good beer.'

This claim was based on the remarkable life of relative Thomas Aitken from Blantyre, who had emigrated from Scotland to Australia in 1842. He set up a brewery in Geelong in 1851 before establishing the much larger, impressively towered Victoria Brewery in East Melbourne in 1854. At the time local 'colonial' breweries had a poor reputation. Aitken helped to change that. His brewery became known for its Victoria Sparkling Ale. He even won medals for his beer in London in 1862 and 1873. In 1907, the Victoria Brewery was one of the founders of Carlton and United Breweries.

Aitken's in Scotland, after two world wars ravaged its foreign trade, also found it could no longer stand alone. Securing outlets at home was proving a struggle despite winning the prestigious Championship Cup for its light cask beer in 1921. It only owned around fifty pubs, largely relying on a widespread free trade, having bought the North Port Brewery in Brechin in 1910, the Rothbury Brewery in Northumberland in 1911 and then TY Paterson of Edinburgh in 1936.

As stronger takeover tides ripped through the industry, Aitken's was absorbed in 1960 by the aggressively expanding Northern Breweries, which had combined a number of Scottish breweries under the United Caledonian banner. Aitken's was now just one of many brands swilling around the bloated group and, as brewing plants were rationalised, famous names were squeezed together.

Falkirk brewery worker Alex Young later recalled that,

> At one time I was bottling for four breweries – Paterson's, Murray's, Fowler's and George Younger's of Alloa. It was all Aitken's beer and stout with their labels on. Aitken's wee heavies [their strong ale] was brewed at 100 gravity and was nearer 90 by the time it was bottled. Fowler's on the other hand was very sweet, but the gravity was brought up by adding priming [sugar].

It rankled the worker to see Aitken's pure principles no longer being upheld. 'Aitken's was one of the very few firms that brewed stout. In fact there was four different qualities. Most pubs had it on draught. We had a large turnover in firkins. Most other breweries converted beer into stout by adding colour, priming and stout caramel, but most of all they used up ullages and returned beer.'

Aitken's even produced a Brussels Stout. 'It was like treacle and deadly, but so was the Export beer. Two pints of any of them would see anybody's boots off,' Young claimed. 'Most of the cellarmen had moustaches and you always knew when they had a go at the stout. Their tongues were always out licking their moustaches.'

Soon the taste would be a distant memory. The brewery closed in 1967 and the site was cleared for an Asda supermarket. Army engineers had to be brought in to demolish the towering 180-foot chimney. Aitken's beers were discontinued, though Tennent's of Glasgow did briefly revive Aitken's 80/- in 1995.

But on the other side of the world, Thomas Aitken's majestic buildings are still a landmark in Melbourne's Victoria Parade, though they ceased brewing in 1983. And Victoria Bitter is the best-selling beer in Australia – bigger than Foster's.

ODD BUT TRUE: In 1877 Bass tried to get Aitken's use of the large red letter A on their labels banned, arguing it looked like the Burton brewer's red triangle trademark. The case was dismissed.

BEER: Deuchar's Export
BREWER: Robert Deuchar, Duddingston Brewery, Edinburgh
ALSO KNOWN FOR: Hampden Roar Malt Ale
BREWERY LOGO: A thistle or the entwined letters of RD Ltd
HISTORIC RIVAL: Aitchison's Export from Edinburgh
SIMILAR BREWS TODAY: Belhaven 80/- from Dunbar
ILLUSTRATIONS: 155, 156, 208-10

DEUCHAR'S EXPORT: Tap into Deuchar's history and you find yourself holding a hazy glass. The more you peer into its depths, the more distorted your vision becomes. And that's before you've drunk a pint or swallowed a press release. Take one incident.

In 1991 the Caledonian Brewery in Edinburgh launched a new beer called R&D Deuchar's IPA. It was another welcome addition to the range of ales produced by the historic Victorian plant, with its direct-fired open coppers, since the site was rescued from closure in 1987 by a management buyout. Scottish crime writer Ian Rankin, the creator of Inspector Rebus, was impressed. 'I was introduced to Deuchar's IPA at the Oxford Bar in Edinburgh, which happens to be Inspector Rebus's local. I don't think I've ever had a bad pint. It's one of our great national drinks.'

There was just one puzzle for Inspector Rebus. Caledonian on Slateford Road had been the former Lorimer & Clark brewery, later owned by Vaux of Sunderland. It had been known for its 70/-, sold as Lorimer's Best Scotch in England, and Golden Strong Ale. It had no connection with the Deuchar brewing brothers. Both Robert and James Deuchar's rival businesses had been taken over by Newcastle Breweries in the 1950s. If anyone still owned the right to the Deuchar name, it was Scottish & Newcastle.

The Scotsman beer columnist Allan McLean called Caledonian's new pale, hoppy brew 'a bit cheeky'. It was cheeky because Caledonian had nipped in to steal the brand after S&N had failed to protect it. The IPA was at first called 'R&D Deuchars' because it was introduced as a trial brew. R&D stood for Research and Development!

By using the Deuchar name, the brave venture was sticking its tongue out at Scotland's brewing giant. And Deuchar's IPA went on to become Caledonian's best-seller. It was so successful, S&N eventually bought the brewery – which was no surprise since the group had a long history of snapping up 'Deuchars'.

Caledonian had launched Deuchar's IPA to boost trade in England. They hoped the name would strike a chord south of the border. For the original Deuchar brothers had made their fortunes not in Scotland, but in and around Newcastle.

According to local legend, teenager James Deuchar arrived on Tyneside with only two shillings in his pocket in the 1860s. He became the landlord of the Argyle Hotel in Gateshead, then the Ridley Arms in Newcastle, which had its own brewery. He went on to buy Allisons' Monkwearmouth Brewery in Sunderland in 1890 and formed James Deuchar Ltd in 1894, adding many prominent pubs and hotels.

Only a few years before his death in 1928, aged seventy-eight, did the business fully venture back into Scotland, buying Ross's Lochside Brewery in Montrose. Monkwearmouth then closed with 'Lochside Ales' shipped down by its own steamer to England. 'The beer boat', as it was known, unloaded at Deuchar's private dock on Newcastle's quayside.

By then James Deuchar was a very rich man. According to Brian Bennison's book, *Brewers & Bottlers of Newcastle*, he was thought to be the largest farmer in Northumberland, owning 7,000 acres, but lived over the border at Stichill House, near Kelso, on a further 6,000 acres. On his death, he left an estate worth more than £1.2 million.

His older brother Robert Deuchar also came to North East England from Forfar as a young man and found the beer trade to his taste, eventually buying Arnison's Sandyford Stone Brewery in Newcastle in 1892 and forming Robert Deuchar Ltd in 1897. But he headed back over the border earlier than James – thanks to a celebrated collapse.

Another pair of booze brothers, Robert and Walter Pattison from Leith, also got a big kick out of alcohol – but in their case it was whisky blending. At one stage their company was seen as a serious rival to Dewar's and Teacher's. Their eye-catching advertising was everywhere, as was news of their extravagant lifestyles. But far too much whisky was being produced and the market crashed in the late 1890s. The Pattisons were later found to be trading fraudulently and both were jailed.

Robert Deuchar could afford to smile over spilt Scotch. Before their collapse, the Pattisons had been hedging their bets by adding beer to their whisky business. Robert Deuchar was able to pick up their new Duddingston Brewery in Edinburgh in 1898 for a knock-down price.

In 1900 the company also bought Simson & McPherson, which ran the St Mary's Brewery in Edinburgh and the Abbey Brewery in Melrose. Both were soon shut with production concentrated at Duddingston. Deuchar's Sandyford Brewery in Newcastle was also later closed.

From the 1920s both James and Robert Deuchar were Scottish brewers – but with their company headquarters in Newcastle, where the bulk of their trade was concentrated. James Deuchar sold its beers under the Lochside brand, notably Lochside Best Scotch on draught and bottled Brown, Pale and Export. Robert Deuchar relied on the family name to promote its beers, particularly Deuchar's Duddingston or Edinburgh Export.

Their success – and large number of pubs on Tyneside – inevitably attracted attention from the dominant local brewer. After Robert Deuchar's son Farquar died in 1947, the business was owned by trustees, who in 1953 accepted a £1 million offer from Newcastle Breweries for the company and its 360 pubs. Newcastle's chairman James Porter, who as head brewer had introduced the famous Newcastle Brown Ale in 1927, followed up three years later by buying James Deuchar with its 125 houses.

James Deuchar's brewery in Montrose quickly closed, though there was a Scotch chaser to its history. It continued in spirit after its death. In 1957 the Lochside Brewery was converted into Macnab's Lochside Distillery and only finally shut in 1992. It was a fitting end for a company once known for marketing its own Squire's Best whisky.

Robert Deuchar's Duddingston Brewery in Edinburgh continued in production until Newcastle Breweries merged with Scottish Brewers (William Younger's and McEwan's) to form Scottish & Newcastle in 1960. The Deuchar name, once such a potent title on Tyneside and in Scotland, was washed away – until the Caledonian Brewery decided drinkers were still 'due a Deuchars'.

ODD BUT TRUE: In a flamboyant flight of fancy, the Pattisons were said to have distributed grey parrots to their pubs – trained to squawk the praises of their whisky and short-lived ales.

BEER: Disher's Ten Guinea Ale
BREWER: Edinburgh United Breweries
ALSO KNOWN FOR: Ritchie's Scotch Ale
BREWERY LOGO: A rampant lion above a thistle
HISTORIC RIVAL: Fowler's Twelve Guinea Ale from Prestonpans

SIMILAR BREWS TODAY: Traquair House Ale, Innerleithen, Peebleshire. While Edinburgh United is a dark tragedy, Traquair House is a warming tale of rare revival. When Peter Maxwell Stuart, the 20th Laird of Traquair, inherited the oldest inhabited house in Scotland, he discovered a centuries-old neglected domestic brewhouse - and decided to bring it back to life in 1965. Surprisingly, the copper - installed in 1739 - was still watertight, while the wooden vessels, which had shrunk from disuse, were restored with a good soaking. His rich, dark Traquair House Ale (7%), first produced with the help of Sandy Hunter from the Belhaven Brewery of Dunbar, is in the 'wee heavy' tradition, with much of the bottled brew now exported.
ILLUSTRATIONS: 157, 158, 211-15

DISHER'S TEN GUINEA ALE: Many breweries are fondly remembered after they have gone. Others are less lamented. But only one has been buried in an unmarked grave as if it never existed.

Once if you mentioned Edinburgh United in older brewing circles, you received a cold stare, tight lips and the conversation swiftly switched to the weather. Yet United's flagship strong ale, the expensively-named Disher's Ten Guinea, was once lauded as 'The Burgundy of Scotland'. Trade in the UK flowed as far as London and Cardiff, while exports sailed to India and New Zealand.

Edinburgh pubs like MacPherson's elaborate Victorian bar in St Leonard's proudly proclaimed on the large windows either side of the entrance 'Disher's Ten Guinea Ale in Bottle', taking precedence over other notable brews like Dalkeith and Bass on smaller windows further down the street. It was a name to tempt drinkers inside.

The extravagant title came from the Scottish system of grading beer based on the gross invoice price for a barrel after 1880, when beer duty replaced the malt and sugar tax. Mostly this was counted in shillings. Thus weak table beer could be as low as 28/-, milds and light ales ranged from 40 to 60/-, while stronger pale and export ales were known as 70 or 80/-. But the most potent, powerful ales were too rich for mere shillings or even pounds. They counted their quality in guineas. George Younger of Alloa produced a Three Guinea Ale; McLennan & Urquart of Dalkeith a Four Guinea. Some brewers like Fowler's of Prestonpans even outbid Disher's with a Twelve Guinea.

These highly priced ales were highly prized. Popularly known as 'wee heavys', they were usually only sold in nips (third-of-a-pint bottles). Many drinkers preferred them as a chaser after a pint or two of standard beer to a glass of whisky. But the taxing reason behind the beer's name was later to come back and haunt Edinburgh United to death.

United was a major venture. It had been launched in an alcoholic haze of ambition in 1889, amalgamating four Edinburgh breweries – Robert Disher's Edinburgh and Leith Brewery, McMillan's Summerhall Brewery, Nicholson's Palace Brewery and the prime mover – George Ritchie and Sons' Bell's Brewery. In many ways it was ahead of its time, having a variety of interests from restaurant and lodging house keepers to farming, dairymen, ice merchants and even brick-makers and bath-keepers.

But the problem was its financial structure never washed. It needed many more guineas in its accounts. It was over-capitalised from the outset and was always under strain, particularly as it relied heavily on the free trade, having only a limited number of pubs. No dividends were paid on its shares for fourteen years from 1903 to 1917. And after the First World War all production was concentrated at Ritchie's brewery to cut costs.

On 21 February 1934, the *Edinburgh Evening Dispatch* carried the headline 'Edinburgh Company Sensation'. It revealed that 'yesterday without previous warning the Excise authorities presented a demand for instant payment of over £51,000'. United could not afford this huge sum. With excise officers having seized all their equipment, paralysing operations, the company immediately applied for liquidation. But there was worse to come. It was not just a case of falling behind with tax payments.

It transpired there had been 'fraudulent evasion of duty' dating back to 1926. Four brewery officials were charged: managing director William Lawrie, head brewer John Clark, assistant brewer David Smith and working brewer Ernest Wiles. Charges against the latter two were later dropped in return for giving evidence for the prosecution.

During the lengthy trial it emerged that United had been secretly brewing at the weekends, with no record of these extra brews kept in the official books. It was a well-organised conspiracy backed up by inaccurate accounts. The court even heard of a secret window to spot approaching excisemen and how stocks of undeclared beer were moved around the brewery to avoid detection. United also sometimes ran off regular brews before they had been assessed for duty. Excise officers had noticed one incident in 1932, but the brewery claimed this was accidental and escaped with a £50 fine.

United's downfall began late in 1933 when they made the fatal mistake of sacking head cellarman Mr Sinclair. Angry at losing his job, the bitter worker exposed the evasion. Excise officers later conservatively estimated that more than 10,000 barrels had been produced free of tax. Many believe it was much more, but records recording the brews had been destroyed.

After ten months in the dock, Lawrie and Clark were found guilty on 14 March 1935 and sentenced to twenty-one months and twelve months in jail respectively. The liquidator, who had briefly resumed brewing, sold the business to rival Edinburgh brewers, John Jeffrey. Brewing ceased. A highly embarrassed industry, fearful that the finger of suspicion might point elsewhere, just wanted to slam the books shut on this damaging episode.

Disher's Ten Guinea Ale had lost its sparkle. The tarnished United name is only still remembered on a few gilded mirrors in Edinburgh bars, though Jeffrey's retained the Disher's name as an extra-strong ale brand until 1960.

ODD BUT TRUE: United's troubled brewery on the Pleasance later housed Edinburgh University's Psychology Department.

BEER: Oatmalt Stout
BREWER: Maclay's of Alloa, founded in 1830 when James Maclay leased the Mills Brewery, before in 1870 building the Thistle Brewery nearby
ALSO KNOWN FOR: 60/- Light and 80/- Export
BREWERY LOGO: A thistle
HISTORIC RIVAL: Oat Creme from Robert Younger of Edinburgh
SIMILAR BREWS TODAY: The Clockwork Beer Company occasionally brews Oat Malt Stout, after Maclay Inns took over the Glasgow brewpub. Sleeman Breweries in Ontario, Canada, has also brewed the stout under licence.
ILLUSTRATIONS: 159, 216, 217

OATMALT STOUT: Oats not only make your morning porridge. As a major crop north of the border, they also inevitably found their way into Scottish beer. And Maclay's of Alloa were best known for sliding this healthy grain into the drinker's tankard, notably in their Oatmalt Stout.

It was a long and proud tradition. Maclay's had won a prize medal for their stout, brewed from malted oats, in 1894 at the International Exposition of Economical Food in Vienna. A bottle label claimed it was 'most nourishing and strengthening' and 'strongly recommended for invalids'. The claims were backed up by an 1895 royal patent from Queen Victoria, granting them exclusive rights to the style.

Oats were big business in Scotland, with more than five million tons produced a year just after the Second World War. Elizabeth Ewing wrote in *Sport & Country* magazine in 1949 that 'the chief secret of the goodness of Scottish oatmeal and rolled oats, and of their sweet, nutty flavour, is the traditional process of kiln-drying'. Malting intensified this effect. In stout this gave a soothing, velvety texture on the tongue. It was a dark dose of liquid porridge in a glass.

Maclay's Viennese waltz with fame was to have an immediate impact at the brewery. James Maclay's sons, James and John, who had inherited the business in 1875, decided to cash in, selling up to a family firm of grocers and grain merchants, the Frasers from Dunfermline, in 1896. The following year Alexander Fraser registered the brewery as a limited company under the name Maclay & Co. Ltd, with a capital of £75,000.

As one of the smaller brewers in Alloa, trade was mainly in central Scotland with some outlets in North East England. But the new company was looking to expand. In 1901 a depot was opened in London's Old Kent Road, supplied by ship from Leith, along with a pub at the Elephant & Castle. Exports went further afield to Ireland, Malta and India, though trade was disrupted by a major fire at the Thistle Brewery in 1910.

Oatmalt Stout was one of the flagship beers, also being supplied to local Alloa rivals Blair's and Meiklejohn's. A 1914 price list shows it selling at 63/- a barrel, more than Export Ale (60/-), Double Brown Stout (54/-) and Pale India Ale (48/-). Only Strong Ale was more expensive at 84/-. During the First World War, owing to a shortage of barley, an Oatmalt Pale Ale was also brewed and patented. This proved so popular that it continued for a number of years after the conflict.

Many brewers south of the border, like Hammerton of London, Magee's of Bolton and Usher's of Wiltshire, produced oatmeal stouts without using oat malt – but these often contained minimal oats. At Crosswells Brewery in Cardiff head brewer Bob Pritchard later admitted, 'One pound of oatmeal was always added to the mash, which made no difference at all in the brew of 200 barrels, but Excise insisted on it to enable us to use the word oatmeal on the label.'

The inter-war years proved difficult for Maclay's, with no dividend declared from 1926 to 1954. The Second World War saw the brewery bombed out of London, as the Luftwaffe destroyed its depot in 1941. After the war it also sold off its sixteen pubs in North East England to Hammond's of Bradford as it retreated out of England.

But the Thistle was to prove a persistent plant on its home soil. It withstood the chill blast of takeovers that blew through the industry in the 1960s, flattening the larger brewers in Alloa. It was a deep-rooted survivor. Company secretary George King liked to tell visitors in the 1970s that 'the car park over the road used to be George Younger's'. It had become Britain's most northerly independent brewery, with just twenty-seven pubs.

It had also resisted the switch to keg beer and sales of its cask 60/-, 70/- and 80/- ales flourished in pubs like the Southsider in Edinburgh. But Oatmalt Stout was not part of the revival, its healthy marketing having fallen foul of stricter advertising rules in the 1960s. The good drop had been dropped. The brewery itself almost crumbled when the council proposed driving a road through the site in 1989. It narrowly survived when the route was diverted.

Oat Malt Stout rose from the dead in 1992, as Maclay's threw off its reputation for dour conservatism under the new ownership of Evelyn Matthews, a former managing director of Bass. It even produced a raspberry beer, using oat malt in the mash. History repeated itself to welcome its return.

A century after its success in Vienna, it won a silver medal at the International Food Exhibition in London in 1995. It was bottled with the proud slogan 'The only Oat Malt Stout in the world' and promoted with a roaring lion rather than a prickly thistle. Oat malt made up 22% of the grist of the 4.5% strength brew.

The full-flavoured stout was also adopted as a house beer by the Asda supermarket chain under the name Hurly Burly. The title came from the manic chant of the three witches in Shakespeare's Macbeth, and sadly Maclay's battle was almost lost and run.

It announced in 1999 that it was to close the ageing Thistle Brewery to concentrate on running its pubs as Maclay Inns. It bid a fruity farewell to the old brewhouse in August with a German-style bock beer called Bramblebock – flavoured with blackberries.

Maclay's head brewer Duncan Kellock set up the Forth Brewery across town in Alloa to continue brewing Maclay's beers, but it did not prove a success and was taken over by Williams Brothers in 2003 to brew their Fraoch heather ale. Belhaven Brewery of Dunbar took over brewing all Maclay's beers, but Oat Malt Stout was rarely brewed. The beer for invalids limped into oblivion.

ODD BUT TRUE: When Duncan Kellock revived Oat Malt Stout in 1992, he found the original recipe also contained lashings of liquorice and a large amount of linseed oil. *Scotsman* beer writer Allan McLean commented, 'Clearly the Victorian invalids who had been prescribed this beer must have been constipated.' Kellock cut right back on the linseed oil as he didn't want drinkers spending the night in the toilet.

BEER: George Younger's 'Revolver'
BREWER: George Younger of Alloa
ALSO KNOWN FOR: Husky Heavy Export
BREWERY LOGO: A large letter 'Y'
HISTORIC RIVAL: William Younger of Edinburgh
ILLUSTRATIONS: 160-2, 218

GEORGE YOUNGER'S 'REVOLVER': When drinkers think about Younger's Scotch ales, the image in their sparkling eyes is of Father William, the white-bearded, tartan-trousered figure waving his walking stick to promote William Younger's beers from Edinburgh. But once another Younger – George Younger – was holding up people around the world with a symbol much less benign than an elderly man – a gun.

Many were persuaded. George Younger's bottled stout was in such demand in the Straits settlements of Malaya during the rubber boom after 1911, that an agent travelled from Singapore to Alloa with a wad of money. He feared the brewery was withholding supplies because it doubted his financial standing. 'He had not realised that stout for export had to mature in cask for a year before bottling,' said a company history in 1925.

George Younger started brewing in Alloa in 1762 at the small Meadow Brewery, but it was not until the family leased the larger Candleriggs Brewery in 1852, finally bought in 1871, that it could expand. But it was already exporting before 1850, notably supplying Demerara with a strong ale in stone bottles. 'Although this ale exceeded 1115 in gravity [11% alcohol],' the firm recalled, 'the consumer in the West Indies did not consider this strong enough and a glass of neat rum had to be mixed with every bottle'.

George Younger might not have quite had the financial muscle of his namesake William, but the brewery was the pride of Alloa, a small port on the Firth of Forth with a big name for beer, boasting eight breweries as well as two distilleries.

Alfred Barnard could not resist the lure of the town's reputation when compiling *Noted Breweries of Great Britain and Ireland* in the 1880s. 'It was with feelings of great delight that we boarded the steamer at Leith for our sail up the Forth to the "Burton of Scotland" … determined to fathom the mystery of "Alloa Ale" … its renown attributed to the purity of the water and the quality of the malt manufactured in the town.'

George Younger was the largest brewing company in Scotland outside Edinburgh. Besides the Candleriggs Brewery, it owned three maltings, including the Craigward complex. But the clue to its trading success lay in its export bottling stores, extending along the shores of the Forth for half-an-acre with their own private wharf.

'Anticipating the demand in an incredibly short time,' said Barnard, 'they had succeeded in placing their East India pale and bitter ales in the foreign markets, until they were in such demand as to necessitate an extension of premises.' On his visit, new fermenting rooms were being built to increase fermenting capacity to 2,500 barrels.

One extensive beer store was called the 'wilderness cellar'. Barnard was impressed by the three domed mash tuns, each with a capacity of 100 quarters, and four coppers, 'two of them imposing vessels, the largest we have seen in Scotland'. Each had a capacity of 150 barrels. The smallest forty-five-barrel copper was used for porter, matured in three vats.

Barnard was entranced by the quick-fingered workers in the export bottling stores.

The fillers sit in front of what looks like a key-board, and the deft way in which they manipulate the bottles, so that none of the precious liquid is wasted, the rapidity with which they pass them on to the corkers, is wonderful to behold.

The centre of the floor of this building is covered with a vast number of butts, filled with Messrs Younger & Son's famous export beer, which is specially brewed for hot climates. Parallel with this bottling store there is another building two storeys high ... the ground floor is filled with matured stock export ales, ready to take the place of those in the bottling house, whilst the upper one is the packing loft, and is also used for storing labels bearing the well-known trade mark 'The Revolver Brand'.

The aggressive image of a gun had helped to shoot George Younger to prominence in foreign markets, notably firing trade in North America and with the military throughout the British Empire. An early label for Revolver Ale showed troopers shooting down spear-carrying natives. Sales abroad went with a bang.

At home, George Younger in 1889 bought Fenwick's breweries in Sunderland and Chester-le-Street with some sixty pubs to protect its substantial sales of Scotch ales in North East England. Thirty years later it added George White's pubs in Newcastle.

In 1919 it also took a half share in the Low, Robertson whisky distillery in Leith. But the same year, it hedged its bets. Worried by the growing power of the temperance movement in Scotland, George Younger bought the former Bass Crest Brewery in Alloa to produce non-alcoholic beers under the 'Pony' brand.

More significantly in 1903 it installed a pioneering carbonation and filtration plant at its Killiebank bottling stores. Within three years bottled sales had trebled thanks to these 'sparkling ales', prompting the setting up of a home bottling department at Eglinton in 1912. Younger also began to make its own bottles from 1908. This was so successful that it was floated as a separate company in 1919, becoming the Scottish Central Glass Works.

But the bullets and bombs of the First World War blew large holes in foreign markets, and in the following depression the brewery struggled, despite slogans on its new cone-topped cans in the late 1930s claiming 'the best beer brewed'. The Second World War left the export Revolver brand firing blanks as the last of its overseas trade faded away.

George Younger sold Fenwick's brewery in Sunderland in 1952 to Flower's of Stratford-upon-Avon to finance a new bottling hall and in 1959 took over local rival, Blair's of Alloa. But trade was poor and only a year later George Younger was itself taken over by Northern Breweries, along with many other famous Scottish breweries.

Rationalisation rapidly followed with the brewery closing in 1963, much to the shock of local people who regarded Younger as the standard bearer of the town's brewing industry. Stormy public meetings followed, but Candleriggs was still snuffed out.

ODD BUT TRUE: There's still one sweet reminder of George Younger surviving today in Sweetheart Stout, now produced by Tennent Caledonian of Glasgow. The bottles and cans still carry the name Younger of Alloa and the girl promoting the brew has not changed in more than fifty years. The smiling face belongs to Hollywood starlet Venetia Stevenson, who first appeared on labels in 1958.

BEER: Younger's No. 3
BREWER: William Younger of Edinburgh
ALSO KNOWN FOR: Tartan, Monk Export and Younger's IPA
BREWERY LOGO: Father William, but also a triple triangle and Holyrood Palace
HISTORIC RIVAL: Robert Younger's Old Edinburgh Ale
SIMILAR BREWS TODAY: Stewart Brewing of Edinburgh, founded in 2004, revived the Scotch legend with Edinburgh No. 3. Then in 2012 Wells & Young's of Bedford, after buying the McEwan and Younger brands, brought back No. 3 as a cask ale.
ILLUSTRATIONS: 163-5, 219, 220

YOUNGER'S No. 3: Many Scottish brewers tried to raid the market over the border, but only one captured the heart of the capital. William Younger was not just Scotland's leading brewer, but also an imposing figure in London with more than fifty prominent pubs in the centre, stretching from The Brompton opposite Harrods in the west to The Ship near the Tower of London in the east.

A 1960s map of its London houses urging drinkers to 'Get Younger every day' boasted, 'If you get weary in Wardour Street, dry in Dean Street, hungry in High Holborn or fatigued in Fish Street Hill ... you can get Younger in two minutes.' In case drinkers didn't get the message, some had a Scottish name like The Holyrood in Oxford Street or The Thistle near Piccadilly Circus. The Tartan army had taken over, decades before Irish bars became all the rage.

And what was the beer at the top of both the draught and bottled beer lists on the map? It wasn't Tartan Bitter or Wee Willie light ale, but No. 3 Scotch Ale. It had originally been called No. 3L, for London. The pubs were known as Scotch houses, and it wasn't just whisky they were talking about.

Journalist Maurice Gorham in his 1949 book *Back to the Local* gave a description of Scotch Ale:

A brown beer rather resembling Burton. In London pubs the term almost invariably stands for Younger's Scotch Ale, in bottle or on draught, which is a genuine Scottish brew. As this is a very popular drink, it is often to be found in free houses, where it usually replaces a Burton ... Younger's Scotch Ale is their No. 3. Their No. 1 is a really strong brew.

Britain's big brewers liked to play the bars by numbers. Bass's No. 1 was their barley wine. Similarly Younger's No. 1 was their strongest ale. But No. 3 was the brew that counted with many drinkers, though that had not always been the score.

William Younger had a sound head for figures. He had founded his brewery at Leith in 1749, but made much of his early income from working as an exciseman. His son Archibald moved operations to Edinburgh in 1778, setting up in the historic grounds of the Abbey of Holyroodhouse. The company became famous for its Edinburgh Ale. 'A potent fluid which almost glued the lips of the drinker together,' according to Chambers' *Traditions of Edinburgh* in 1825, 'and of which few, therefore, could dispatch more than a bottle.' It was a brew in the No. 1 tradition.

The Abbey Brewery expanded and, by the start of the nineteenth century, Younger's was already shipping substantial amounts to London, with exports further afield. In 1858 a larger plant, the Holyrood Brewery, was built nearby to keep up with spiralling demand. William Younger had become a famous name to conjure with – and to forge.

Nicolson, the firm's American agent in St Louis in the late 1850s, had to put an advert in the local papers, stating, 'I would caution the purchasers of Scotch Ale against the many spurious imitations sold ... in this city. To escape prosecution for forgery, they have slightly changed the spelling thus – "Yonkers", while retaining the same style of bottles and colour, and otherwise a facsimile of the genuine label.' There was also confusion with rival Scottish brewers, George Younger of Alloa and Robert Younger of Edinburgh, so in foreign markets the 'Monk' brand was introduced.

Brewery chronicler Alfred Barnard inevitably came knocking on the gates of Scotland's King of Ales (as it called its No. 1 brew) in the late 1880s. His visit stretched over four days in order to see 'two great breweries' and 'an immense range of granaries and maltings'. The historic Abbey Brewery still brewed the potent Edinburgh Ale, while the more modern Holyrood plant was known for its IPA. Both followed the leading Burton breweries in using union casks for cleansing the beer during fermentation. All beer for export was stored for twelve months. Even celebrated French scientist Pasteur had inspected the laboratories. William Younger was Scotland's answer to Bass, in quality and fame.

And Barnard's tour was not complete without later dropping into the company's London stores on the South Bank in railway arches under Hungerford Bridge. In 1932 the depot moved to Princes Wharf in Lambeth and David Keir, in his 1951 book *The Younger Centuries*, recalled one of the dirtier jobs to ensure 1,500 casks could be landed from each barge. 'At low water, when the receding tide leaves a bed of dark sticky mud at Princes Wharf, members of the London staff known as "mudlarks" go out in waders, push the mud's top dressing back into the river with broad wooden rakes, and so keep the wharf's approaches navigable.'

By the 1930s the white-bearded, tartan-trousered figure of Father William, swinging his walking stick, was strolling the streets of London as if he owned them. In some cases he did, given the growing number of Younger pubs in the capital, many refurbished in a distinct mock-Tudor style with tartan tapestries.

Father William was almost a celebrity in his own right, having been designed by artist Alfred Leete, who had created the memorable wartime recruitment poster of finger-pointing Lord Kitchener saying 'Your country needs YOU.' He first appeared in a press advert in 1921 above the lines inspired by *Alice in Wonderland*: 'You are old, Father William, the young man did say. All nonsense my lad, I get Younger each day.'

Father William may have been an old man, but he was capable of new tricks. Late in 1930 the company shocked the industry by announcing a merger with Edinburgh rival William McEwan to form Scottish Brewers, with a new company McEwan-Younger handling the export trade. The combination consolidated Younger's dominant position as the top notch Scotch brewer and it celebrated its anniversary in 1949 with a 'spicy nut-brown ale' called Double Century in the No. 3 tradition.

But south of the border England's major brewers followed Younger's example by forming national combines in the 1960s. The Scottish giant tried to keep ahead of the game by merging with the major brewer in North East England to form Scottish & Newcastle Breweries in 1960. But as it lacked the huge pub numbers owned by the other groups, it also targeted the free trade with a new style of beer.

William Younger had always been a traditional brewer. When others introduced filtered, chilled and carbonated bottled beer, it had at first resisted. David Keir in *The Younger Centuries* said the company 'frowned' on the development, preferring to stick to naturally conditioned bottled beer for the home market. 'It was felt that to process beer in such a manner must inevitably sacrifice some of its goodness and distinctive character.' But when it bowed to pressure and installed a modern bottling plant in 1920, sales of a new lighter ale called Holyrood took off. It was a lesson for the future.

In a supplement in *The Scotsman* in 1962, the company stated that the majority of its draught beer was still sold in traditional wooden oak casks and this was expected to continue 'for many years to come'. But it also mentioned that 'a recent development is the sale of beer in metal drums of 11-gallons capacity. While this is sold as "draught" the ale itself is more akin to bottled beer, being chilled, conditioned and filtered prior to dispatch'. Its great advantage was that it was ready to serve immediately, unlike cask beer, and had proved 'very popular' in golf clubs and theatre bars. Keg beer had arrived and Younger's Tartan and McEwan's Export were soon two of the leading brands.

They were so successful that within little more than a decade cask beer had been rolled into the darkest corner of the cellar and forgotten. Brewing of Younger's No. 3 ceased in 1974, but then was brought back for the London area in 1979, but there was little enthusiasm for the real ale revival, as I discovered on a visit to the Edinburgh company in 1982 for the CAMRA newspaper *What's Brewing*.

> Scottish & Newcastle head of public relations Peter Dundas carefully countered questions about the health of their cask beers like a hospital consultant discussing a dying patient with a relative. Production was static, he believed. There might be slight signs of improvement, but it was minimal ... he shook his head. He thought they brewed about 700 barrels a week. It was the figure they usually quoted.
>
> New group product marketing director, Guy Dixon, said the figure sounded a little low. He took out his pocket calculator and pressed a few buttons. About a thousand barrels a week, he estimated. He was more optimistic. He believed the patient had a future.
>
> Fountain Brewery boss Pat Castle was much more certain about the figures, as you would expect of the production director. They brewed 1,500 barrels of cask beer that week. But in the summer it had been up to 1,800 barrels, peaking at almost 2,000.

This was still only a fair drop in the ocean of processed beers pouring out of the modern Fountain Brewery, built in 1973, but it was more than double the first figure given a few hours before. S&N seemed to have lost belief in their traditional beers, particularly Younger's ales, preferring to promote McEwan's 80/- and then Theakston's real ales, after taking over the North Yorkshire brewery in 1987.

By then Younger's Holyrood Brewery had closed in 1986 – the Abbey Brewery having already been turned into offices in 1955 – with production concentrated at McEwan's Fountain Brewery on the other side of the city. So ended the famous 'Royal Mile of Ale', stretching from Edinburgh Castle to the palace of Holyrood House. This area, blessed with ideal mineral water, had been brewing for centuries since the first monks of Holyrood Abbey. The district around Canongate was once home to more breweries than any other comparable area in the UK. Now the sweet aroma of mashing malt had been blown from the ancient streets. And Younger's No. 3 was to follow.

After buying Courage in 1995 to become the UK's largest brewer, Scottish had many more brands to play with. Younger's No. 3 was not even thirty-third on its list of priorities. The rich, dark drop (4.5% alcohol), which had still been promoted in the 1980s as having a 'distinctive fullness of flavour not found in other beers ... a truly memorable ale', was squeezed out. The final brew was in May 1998. Scotch was on the rocks almost 150 years after the clipper *Alice Walton* sailed to Australia with 50 hogsheads in 1856. The beer welcomed in Sydney after months at sea had finally sunk.

ODD BUT TRUE: The site of Younger's Abbey Brewery is now the home of the Scottish Parliament.

Index
of Beers & Breweries